Interior Joy

"Living Your God *Designed* Life"

An Exciting Journey Transforming
The Interior Spaces

Of Your
Heart and Home.

Charisse Holder

Notes

1. The Holy Bible, New King James Version Giant Print Reference Bible, (Holman Bible Publishers 2013).

2. Avery T. Willis, Jr., The Disciple's Victory, LifeWay Press 1996, 129-131.

3. Michael Townsend, Justpaint.org, Defining Warm and Cool Colors: It's All relative, July 13, 2017.

4. Life Application Bible: New International Version (Tyndale House Publishing, Inc. 1991)

One Smart Lady Productions and Gladstone Publishing Services
Newark, DE 19702

First Edition

Imprint: Gladstone Publishing
ISBN: 978-1-928681-59-5

Printed in United States of America

DEDICATION

I dedicate this book to my Mom, born Katie Delores Pendleton. From the time of our birth to this very day, you have been there for your girls- in mind, body, soul, and now spirit. I have wonderful memories of a beautiful home due to your amazing decorating skills. You were the epitome of what this book is all about; 'Maximizing what you have and doing your best to create an atmosphere of- Interior Joy.' Thank you for being the stellar example of hard work, perseverance, and strength like no other, never-ever giving up. Thank you for instilling the importance of living your truth and doing everything with heart. I love you beyond measure!

ACKNOWLEDGMENTS

To my God- This would not be possible without you. Thank you Lord, I love You!

To my husband, Lou- You're amazing! Thank you for supporting me through each step of this process. Your willingness to patiently assist in all areas helped make this dream possible. I love you dearly!

To my son, Jordan and my daughter, Jasmine- Thank you for being such loving support and willing to assist whenever it was needed. Thank you, Jasmine, for your color-wheel painting contribution and Jordan for your technical skills. I'm so proud of your beautiful souls and hearts for Christ. I love you to the moon and back!

To my sisters Melissa and Yvette- I love you beyond measure. Your support has been invaluable to this process. I can't think of better 'Cheerleaders' providing loving advice, support, and encouragement the entire distance. I'll love you always!

To Mom and Dad, Dr. Neville and Hyacinth Holder- Thank you for always providing love and support through the years.

To Nicole, Nadine, Jim, and Gerard- Thank you for your support and encouragement over the years.

To Sarah, Rachel, and Naomi- Thank you for your hearts for Christ, using your gifts and doing your best as you grow in Him.

To those who assisted in the photography and design- Ethan Gaskin and Kimberly Galeano-Rubio; you are both very talented. Thank you for being so accommodating and willing to share your gifts and talents. You will go far in life due to your genuine heart.

To my family, friends, and village- Thank you! Thank you! The road is never always easy, but the journey towards greater is always worth it! I appreciate your love and support over the years!

To all my clients, I truly appreciate you! Thank you for trusting me with your home and allowing me the opportunity to share this gift. My experience with you has allowed me the knowledge and skill to write this book and the opportunity to now call many of you 'friends.' You all know my heart and spirit, and I pray your home transformation has brought you true- Interior Joy!

To Deborah Smart, Senior Publishing Editor/Consultant for One Smart Lady Productions and Gladstone Publishing Services- Words cannot express the gratitude I have for you and all your hard work. Thank you so much for taking on this project and allowing me to see this dream to the finish line. You have a heart of gold, and I am forever grateful for your giving spirit and all your beautiful work. I wish you much success as you move forward to achieve all that God has in-store for you and your company.

TABLE OF CONTENTS

LAYOUT

To enjoy the process of this book the diagram below is an "At-A-Glance' view of how the book is structured.

	God's Principle	*Décor Principle*
Step 1	The Plan	Décor Plan and Function
Step 2	You-niquely Designed	Décor Style
Step 3	Attitude	Décor Home Mood
Step 4	Strategic Intentions	Décor Color Scheme
Step 5	Use What You Have	Décor Furniture
Step 6	Order	Décor Layout
Step 7	Favor	Décor "Wow Factor"
Step 8	Be The Light	Décor Lighting
Step 9	Whole Armor	Décor Accessories
Step 10	Maximize	Décor Budget/Smart Shop

PREFACE

PURPOSE

Have you ever wondered…."How do I experience all that God has *designed* for me?" "How do I have *joy* in my life and home-right now?"

Home is where the heart is, and that's why I'm so passionate about it. Its atmosphere is more than just décor; it *highlights* the soul and *nourishes* the spirit of you. Whether it's large, small, a rented room, or owned, your home's power and impact can't be underestimated.

We all have a gift to share, and God showed me this one back in 1992. From the moment I discovered my passion for decorating, I knew God had more in store. Thirteen years later my business was registered, and the passion is just as great today!

Now…as a Professional Interior Decorator, I've served hundreds of clients, taught years of decorating courses, and mentored many budding Entrepreneurs; in order to enrich the lives and homes of others. No matter your space, the atmosphere should not only be beautiful but a place of healing, peace, comfort, love, and sharing. Achieving this should be satisfying and enjoyable!

This book is a one-of-a-kind journey through my ten-step decorating process, utilizing powerful biblical principles to transform the interior spaces of your heart while creatively renewing the atmosphere of your home.

As you move through each step, you will gain time tested truths that God has uniquely designed for you. The interior spaces of your heart and home are powerfully interconnected, and maximizing this truth will fully awaken what I call 'INTERIOR JOY'!

I Thessalonians 5:16-18 (NIV)

"Be joyful always; pray continually; give thanks in all circumstances, for this is God's will for you in Christ Jesus"

INTERIOR JOY
What Is It?

In You

Interior joy is an experience of the heart- the place where God resides! It's stable, consistent, firm, and gilded in truth. It gives you peace when the world is chaotic, it coats you in calmness when you want to scream, it's your go-to place when you need a refuge, and it gives you answers when no one else knows.

Not superficial, but instead, so physically real; it keeps you smiling even when you want to cry, keeping you in motion and moving you forward even when the world challenges you along the way. It's a fruit of the spirit, not dependent upon any individual or circumstance. It's always within reach, ready to be awakened when you connect to its presence.

True interior joy is the grace God provides to help you navigate His path—a path beautifully set for you!

In Your Home

Interior joy in the home is an atmosphere created from a heart that puts God first. With a spirit that's open to God and a heightened sense of gratitude, creativity is magnified, producing beautiful spaces. With this greater level of appreciation for what God has entrusted to you, you begin to see the items in your home differently. You will have a new mindset for what you already own, opening the gateway for amazing results!

Reciprocity

This experience formulates a process of reciprocity; all starting and ending with God. As we put God first, gratitude and creativity will then be reflected in our home, which ultimately honors God... flowing full circle.

Joy reciprocated!

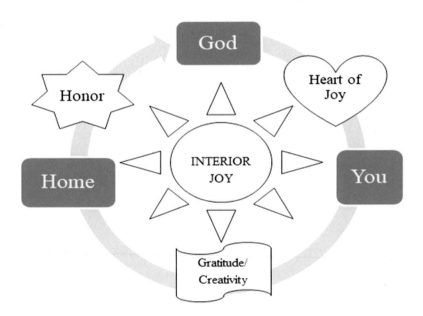

INTRODUCTION
Feeling Stuck

As I write about the interior joy of the home and this process of reciprocity, I think about what has occurred in my own home. Ready to re-decorate after 16 years living in the same design, I felt stuck. Too many other priorities took precedence, and my desire for an updated look in my home weighed heavily on my spirit.

As a professional Interior Decorator, it may seem that changes to my home could occur at any time. However, this is not the case. The changes I desired and needed after 16 years would require significant time and money, even if done on a budget.

My home was beautiful but…beautifully outdated (for me). The carpet on the stairs had become worn, the walls needed painting, all the window treatments and wall art needed updating. It's possible, on average, every 7-10 years, rooms may need some updating, styles change, and so do our likes and dislikes. For most of us, priorities like work, kids, or bills are front and center with an insatiable demand for attention. So, updating a space may have to wait.

After I stopped complaining to myself and showed appreciation for what I did have, I was able to see the changes I could make while waiting for a more extensive overhaul. I pulled the carpet off the stairs and donated items I no longer needed. I began to envision a new look for the stairs that would only require a new coat of paint and some serious elbow grease. Hmmm, I thought…this is going to be great!

After a few weeks of living with the bare sub-floors on my stairs, while waiting for the scheduled day to do something inexpensive to them like painting, it finally happened, my window of opportunity arrived! God perfectly aligned the time and a little money to do the upgrades…it was unexpected, but greatly welcomed. I prayed to let

God know how grateful I was, pulled out my plans (created months earlier), and swiftly moved into action.

I believe God saw my change in attitude months before. My attitude changed, and I was prepared for the moment. I stopped focusing on what I didn't have and focused on what I could do with what I had. Yes, being grateful increased my creativity. With the new focus, God orchestrated all that was needed to make the necessary changes. Once I prayed, changed my attitude from complaints to appreciation, God aligned it all, in His perfect timing, not my own.

This total cycle of reciprocity has now taken place in my home, and I can now write about it. Putting God first awakened my heart to His joy, allowing me to appreciate what I had. This attitude of gratitude increased my creativity in seeing what I could do with what I had at the moment. When I maximized what God already entrusted to me, I was able to then honor Him with my new attitude and, ultimately, my home.

It starts and ends with God!

Before   **After**

Isaiah 65:21-22 (NKJV)

They shall build houses and inhabit them;...For as the days of a tree, so shall be the days of My people, and my elect shall long enjoy the work of their hands.

God's Desire

Did you know God's desire for you is joy at all times? Sounds crazy, right? Well, it's true.

Take a look…

I Thessalonians 5:16 (NKJV)

"Rejoice <u>always</u>, pray without ceasing, in everything give thanks; for this is the will of God in Christ Jesus for you."

I Peter 1:8 (NKJV)

"Thou now you do not see Him, yet believing you rejoice with joy inexpressible and full of glory, receiving the end of your faith-the salvation of your soul."

Philippians 4:4-8 (NKJV)

"Rejoice in the Lord always. Again I will say rejoice".

These commands are just scratching the surface to the many times we are told to rejoice and be grateful.

The joy referenced here is true 'interior joy', joy everlasting, not a temporary spark, but an eternal flame!

It can never be quenched no matter how rough things get. God wants rejoicing to be a lifestyle, not just a momentary idea. With Christ, not only is it possible, it's already done!

John 15:11 (NKJV)

"These things I have spoken to you, that My joy may remain in you, and that your joy may be full."

The world wants you to believe everlasting joy is not possible, but it is. God says so!

The joy of God resides within all believers. It is the gift that He has given you, placing the seed of himself, eternity, in the heart of every man.

Ecclesiastes 3:11 (NKJV)

"He has made everything beautiful in its time. Also, He has put eternity in their hearts, except that no one can find out the work that God does from beginning to end."

Romans 5:5 (NKJV)

"Now hope does not disappoint, because the love of God has been poured out in our hearts by the Holy Spirit who was given to us.

All that God has done, we cannot fathom, just believe, and receive. Interior Joy is possible, at all times, because of Christ!

Pruning for Joy

Having interior joy does not mean that you will never feel sadness, or you won't be treated unfairly. It means within your core; your heart-joy will always bring you back to your center and remind you of the truth.

Facts and truths are not the same.

Facts are what may be present in the physical limitations of this world, but truth is… immeasurable possibilities ignited by faith and orchestrated by God.

A fact may be that a personal goal was not achieved or you feel a friend alienated you, but the truth is... personal setbacks are the pruning tools needed for your growth; and challenges in relationships may be used by God to get you to depend on Him, not man.

When you focus on truth, not just facts, you learn that pruning will take place even for followers of Christ. He will prune to produce more fruit!

John 15:2 (NKJV)

"He cuts off every branch in me that bears no fruit, while every branch that does bear fruit he prunes, so that it will be even more fruitful."

Did you see that? The branch that does bear fruit is pruned so that it will be even more fruitful. There is a difference between cutting and pruning. Cutting is to remove it all, and pruning is done to stimulate internal growth!

God cuts off the entire branch that bears no fruit; he gets rid of it entirely. However, the branch that actually bears good fruit remains, but is still pruned. To prune is to keep the branch but remove the dead infected or diseased portion of the branch. Pruning removes what's unproductive to stimulate productive growth for increase.

Pruning Produces Productivity!

Romans 5:3 (NKJV)

"And not only that, but we also glory in tribulations, knowing that tribulation produces perseverance; and perseverance, character; and character, hope."

Until you know truth, you will mistake a life challenge that was meant for pruning and view it as failure. Without knowing truth, these challenges will constantly derail you and your life will be full of heartache. Instead of heartache experience the "heart-change" God has purposed for you.

Psalm 56:4 (NKJV)

"I trust in God, so why should I be afraid? What can mere mortals do to me?"

When you connect with the source of truth and joy, you know that everything that happens in your life happens with a purpose. These 'negative happenings' are the pruning that is part of the solution, not the problem. Once you grasp this, your focus will begin to shift, and you will recognize the ever-present joy. Your valuable time, energy, mind, and strength will be properly placed towards what's most important.

God's destiny is waiting for you, and you don't have time to waste on unimportant things that don't ultimately matter. God's pruning is to remove these unimportant, distracting, diseased parts of your branch and keep you focused on the healthy branches that generate interior joy!

Romans 8:28 (NKJV)

"And we know that all things work together for good to them that love God, to them who are called according to his purpose."

My Journey in 1992

My house was small but beautiful, just enough space for one, maybe two. There was a small yet elegant and very unexpected spiral staircase gracing the front entry. Don't get me wrong, this was no large, grand staircase, but it was perfect for me. The décor was warm and inviting; creatively designed by yours truly. I was at the height of my sales career, enjoying my space and loving life! It was all in place-the career I desired, excelling and winning top honors and awards at work, I had more than enough money to take care of my needs and then some, there was money in the bank and long term investments, company car, expense account, five-star meals in restaurants, the works!

One day, I walked down my beautiful spiral staircase, looked outside my back door, over the expansive deck in my back yard, and sighed-feeling this bold yet sinking feeling in the pit of my stomach-thinking to myself. "Is this it? There has to be more to life than this. I'm missing something."

But wait...I had everything, which by the world's standard would bring most people great happiness. However, although I was happy, I felt something missing. The more intrinsic joy seemed to evade me. At the very least, I wanted someone, a significant other, to share my life and all these 'things' with. Up until this point, I did not have a desire to have children after marriage, but for some reason, I now began to consider having children once I met the right man and got married.

I was 26 years old, single, and now at a stage in life where I recognized that I no longer wanted 'the pursuance of money' as my only motivator! I currently had all the "stuff" that I needed in my life. Although I was young and loving life, I was a saved soul; two years into my recommitted, Christ-focused life.

So, after having all this <u>and</u> a Christ-focused life, why did I still feel this void? Why didn't I have the happiness or correction, 'the joy' I should have been experiencing? Looking back on this time in my life, now in my 50's, and having the hindsight of someone who's now much wiser, I have determined the answer. Although God was a major part of my life, I wasn't focused on what truly created joy. I wasn't at a mature stage in my walk for renewed thinking. Maturity in your walk with Christ is not dependent upon your age; you can be a mature Christian at a young age, as long as you are growing and applying God's word. So yes, I was young and determined to be successful. You know…success as "they" define success to be. Who is "they" anyway?

The fact was, I had everything that should bring happiness; however, because God was on board, he began to re-direct my focus to truth. He showed me that even though I had a lot of external "stuff," he had greater things in store. He helped me to see that the void was not a lack of God in my life but a lack of understanding and application of God's principles and truth. I may have been reading my word, but was I applying them? The fact was, I had all the material "things" of life, but the truth was, I needed to renew my mind and focus on applying God's principles, not the principles of the world.

Romans 12:2 (NKJV)

"And be not conformed to this world, but be ye transformed by the renewing of your mind, that ye may prove what is that good, acceptable, and perfect, will of God.

The world will have you thinking that material things and other people, a new house, or a new spouse will bring you joy. Oh no, that's a trap, a set up for disappointment.

It's crazy; we can have God on board and still be lost?!! If all we do is read the word and not gain understanding by being intentional and applying His principles, we are still lost! Faith without works is dead!

James 2:14 (NKJV)

"What does it profit, my brethren, if someone says he has faith but does not have works? Can faith save him?"

If you're doing well with all the material things life has to offer, but still feel a void in your life, it may be that you need God or more time with Him, in His word and applying His principles. You need a renewing of your mind. God helped me to understand that "things" should never be the source of my happiness, and it definitely will not be the source of my joy. 'Things' can be taken at a moment's notice. If you're feeling a void, you may need to connect or reconnect and 'apply' His principles.

Interior joy is what is 'awakened', not just sparked when we:
- ✓ **Connect with God.**
- ✓ **Be thankful always.**
- ✓ **Understand truth.**
- ✓ **Appreciate Pruning.**
- ✓ **Apply His Principles.**

✓ **Interior Joy Check – Introduction**

1. Have you given your life to Christ? Pray and share your thoughts with God.

2. What has resonated with you most about the meaning of interior joy?

3. What, about your home, can you be more grateful for today?

Step 1

The Plan

God's Principle

STEP 1

GOD'S PLAN

God created us all for His ultimate purpose. He made us and He loves us. There!...it's that simple- our purpose is to live in God's image and likeness bearing fruit for His ultimate glory and purpose.

However, how we live-out that purpose is unique to each one of us. It's impossible to live your purpose without God. When you accept Jesus Christ, the Holy Spirit is deposited in you, guiding you along your life's journey.

Ephesians 1:9-12 (NKJV)

> *"...having made known to us the mystery of His will, according to His good pleasure which He purposed in Himself... In Him also we have obtained an inheritance, being predestined according to the purpose of Him who works all things according to the counsel of His will, that we who first trusted in Christ should be to the praise of His glory."*

Isaiah 43:21 (NKJV)

> *"This people I have formed for Myself; They shall declare My praise."*

Genesis 1:27 (NKJV)

> *"So God created man in His own image; in the image of God, He created him; male and female He created them."*

Romans 8:29 (NKJV)

"For whom He foreknew, He also predestined to be conformed to the image of His Son, that He might be the firstborn among many brethren."

Living your life each day knowing you were created by God, with a plan and a purpose in mind, is interior joy. Your ultimate destiny becomes possible once you begin to understand this truth and learn how to be guided by God's principles for your life. Are you on track to fulfilling God's destiny for you? Understand that your life is about the journey which ultimately leads to your destiny.

Destiny is the treasure, but the jewel is in the journey.

Interior Joy originates from God, whose presence lies within. It's the discovery of God's intention for you; to know his plans for you, understand why he sent his Son for you, and to exercise the great power he's given you through his Son. All of this grace has been provided *to* you and, ultimately, *for* God's glory!

Psalm 16:11 (NKJV)

*"Thou wilt show me the path of life: in thy presence is **fullness of joy**; at thy right hand there are pleasures forevermore."*

I will pray that if you haven't given your life to Christ up to this moment in time, you will seriously seek Christ and ask him to rule and reign in your heart. You can't reach your earthly or eternal destiny without a connection to the one who created you.

Gifts

God placed unique gifts in you to use for His ultimate purpose. Yes, you have gifts, and God expects you to use them.

Romans 12:6 (NKJV)

"Having then gifts differing according to the grace that is given to us, let us use them; if prophecy, let us prophesy in proportion to our faith; or ministry, let us use it in our ministering; he who teaches, in teaching, he who exhorts, in exhortation; he who gives, with liberality he who leads with diligence; he who shows mercy, with cheerfulness."

Often times, we waste time trying to figure out our purpose. No need to waste any more time. Your purpose is to honor God. How? Make Jesus the Lord of your life and let Him lead the way! Through connecting and communing with God, you will discover the plans he has set for you. He will direct your path and help you identify the gifts He has entrusted to you. You can then take those gifts, talents, and abilities, share them with others, and lead others to Christ! We must stop procrastinating and complicating what God has already revealed in His word.

Jeremiah 29:11 (NKJV)

"For I know the thoughts that I think toward you, says the Lord, thoughts of peace and not of evil, to give you a future and a hope."

We search and search for meaning. We are confused as to our purpose and our destiny. There is no reason to be lost. You must seek the answers from the one who lovingly created you. God desires for you to connect with him so badly that He gave his only Son so that you can directly commune with him, and get ALL of your questions answered. God is too obvious to deny, and so is His love for you!

Step 1

The Plan

Décor Principle

STEP 1

DÉCOR PLAN AND FUNCTION

God's plan and purpose are for us to live a life that glorifies Him, day-by-day building character to become more like Jesus. How you live in your home matters. The Christ-like character of you outside your home should be built and nourished inside your home. Your home's physical atmosphere plays a vital role in this process. How it functions, looks and supports your life must first start with

A PLAN.

Decorating should be an enjoyable experience. Some may enjoy it more than others, but don't let the fun of it all cause you to move too fast in the process and purchase a lot of things without a plan. Just as God created the world with a plan and order, decorating a space in your home requires a plan. Without a plan, you will move out of order nd the results are never as good as you intended.

This is one of the biggest mistakes many people make when decorating their homes. They get excited about the process without first creating a plan. You know how we do, hit the stores running and gathering all the "pretty stuff" that catches our eye. We then take it home and it doesn't quite have the look and feel we desired. We may use it for a while, but then it happens…It eventually moves to the pile of never-never land, the pile of forgotten clutter. Sounds familiar?

Well, clutter no more, and your design plan will help the process. Your plan will eventually include all of the ten steps we will discuss in this journey to Interior Joy in our home and life. It is such an important step. Its purpose is to keep you on track with the vision of the space and not get side-tracked by all the 'pretty stuff' in the stores. I am a huge fan of the wonderful discount furnishing stores now available online and through brick and mortar locations. We live in a wonderful time where so much is available to us. Just 5 years ago, most of these great options were not in existence.

To start the plan for your space, you must first determine:
- ✓ **What room are you creating? I say creating, because you may be transforming a dining room into an office or a bedroom into a closet.**
- ✓ **What is the purpose and how will the room function?**
- ✓ **What are the main activities that will take place?**
- ✓ **Who will use it every day?**

This is the first item to determine for your plan. Purpose and function comes before the décor style.

When working with clients, many will try to decorate based on one or two large parties they may or may not have within the year. I like to explain that it is important to decorate your space based on who lives there every day and who will be using the space the most. There is no need to purchase 15 dining chairs, even for a large formal, space if only four people live in the house daily. When you have a large gathering, you can pull other chairs from other spaces into the room or use temporary folding chairs if needed. You can save a lot of time and money focusing on your everyday use instead of the big party that may only happen every other year.

If the room will be used mainly by children below the age of 5, child safety measures will need to be considered. If elderly members of the household are its main users, sofas, and chairs with a higher seat level for easy standing is important. Even possibly removing area rugs to avoid tripping and nasty falls are key.

If the space being decorated is the **family room** and the family will be the everyday users, consider the activities that will take place. Do you enjoy family games or movie watching? Maybe a table for fun activities and a large sectional sofa is exactly what's needed. The remaining nine steps to decorating your space can not take place until this foundational step is completed. As we move throughout this book, we will take the journey of transforming this 'Family Room'.

FAMILY ROOM

Our Design Plan
Step 1
Room & Function

Family Room. Relaxed, casual fun. T.V. viewing, napping, games, reading, homework. Everyday users-Two adults. Two kids. No pets.

✓ **Step 1 Interior Joy Check - The Plan**

1. Select one space in your home you would like to decorate. How would you like it to function? What are the activities that will take place there most often?

2. Stand in the space and thank God for every item. Express to Him how grateful you are. Write your thoughts here.

3. With a heightened sense of gratitude, pray for God to reveal how you can re-purpose at least 50% of what you currently have. Think of all the creative, inexpensive things you can do to transform your space. Write it here.

Step 2

Style

God's Principle

STEP 2

'YOU'-NIQUELY DESIGNED

From the beginning, YOU were designed…God designed you even before you were conceived! I don't know about you, but that amazes me! Your creator knew you before your parents knew each other. Our God is so magnificent that every individual was carefully planned, created in His image, and arrived with their very own life-print, unique in every way. Knowing you were designed in God's image and arrived with your own "one-of-a-kind" life print is one of the keys to living your life of Interior Joy!

Jeremiah 1:5 (NKJV)

"Before I formed you in the womb I knew you; before you were born, I sanctified you…"

When you understand that you are purposely designed and one-of-a-kind, you'll then begin to see that you are graced with 'His full blessing'; every tool needed to reach your God-breathed destiny. He put it all in you!

Hebrews 3:17 (NKJV)

"…that the man of God may be complete, thoroughly equipped for every good work."

YOU ARE WORTHY!!! God said so. You are worthy, through Jesus Christ! Don't ever believe otherwise.

To gain the full experience of this book, it is important to bring to the forefront the truth of how special and important you are. You are a JOY to God; that's why he created you! When God created you, He

11

did so because he chose to. In life, it's a beautiful thing to be chosen; to be selected not because someone HAD to select you, but because they CHOSE to select you. This is what God has done for you; He chose to design and birth you out of His LOVE for you!

John 15:16 (NKJV)

"You did not choose Me, But I chose you and appointed you that you should go and bear fruit, and that your fruit should remain, that whatever you ask the Father in My name He may give you."

Yes, God birthed you.

Even though your earthly mother was the vehicle through which you entered the world, you belong to God. Your earthly parents/ guardians, whether biological or not, are expected to do the right thing; raise HIS children to be God-honoring individuals. Even if your earthly parents make wrong choices, God can 'right' those wrongs for His ultimate glory!

Psalm 100:3 (NKJV)

"Know that the Lord is God. It is He, who made us, and we are His, we are His people, the sheep of his pasture."

Although God chose you, you must, at some point, choose God. You cannot reach the destiny He desires for you without doing so. God created you with the unique ability to exercise freedom of choice.

John 15:19 (NKJV)

"If you belonged to the world it would love you as its own. As it is, you do not belong to the world, but I have chosen you out of the world."

Right now, you may not understand why God chose you and why He loves you so much, but that is not required. We do not understand all that God is; for His ways are not our ways.

Proverbs 3:5-6 (NKJV)

"Trust in the Lord with all your heart, and lean not on your own understanding; in all your ways acknowledge Him, and He shall direct your paths."

Isaiah 55:8 (NKJV)

"For my thoughts are not *your thoughts, nor are your ways my ways, says the Lord."*

Now that you know you were chosen and designed even before you were conceived, if you have not done so, it's time for you to choose God. Decide to trust in God and put Him first.

To experience your life of Interior Joy, you must first choose God!

Step 2

Style

Décor Principle

STEP 2

DÉCOR STYLE

Just as God designed and chose you, the next step in your home's decorating plan is choosing your personal design style. Identifying your design style can sometimes be a little tricky. If you are not familiar with the basic elements that define various styles, you may have a challenge pin-pointing a title for your unique flair.

When it comes to style, yours can be as unique as the fingerprint God gave you. There are no major rules to what your style should be, but there are some standard design principles that can be a helpful guide.

Your design is your story to the world, or at least to those who visit your home. Being comfortable with who you are will allow your home to authentically represent the best of you. In essence-it feeds your soul and becomes the refuge from a world too eager to conform to the masses. There should be no concern for what others may be doing in their homes or what others think you should have. Your home represents the unique experience of you.

If you're decorating a home for more than one, it can be a delicate balance. There is a way to produce the right atmosphere that will satisfy everyone. This is why a plan is so important. It helps you to think through all the details and determine the best solution.

Let's take a look at some of the standard styles you may be familiar with. A few include:

Traditional, Transitional, Modern, Contemporary, Industrial, Shabby Chic, Country Farm House, Eclectic. There are more, but we'll focus on these few.

The beautiful thing is, you can coin your very own style according to your personality and flair. Some unique styles I have been asked by clients to create include Ethnic Floridian, Modern Afro-Centric, and Urban Industrial Farmhouse, just to name a few. It is perfectly okay to coin your own style, as a matter of fact, I encourage you to do so!

My signature-style is 'Transitional' with a 'Casual Elegance' mood. I love décor that is relaxing with a touch of elegance. And by the way, we tend to dress in our preferred home styles as well! My daily clothing tends to mimic the same signature-style and mood preferences as my home, colors, and all!

Here are the identifiers for some of the more popular styles listed:

Traditional:

Classic shapes and patterns. Withstand the test of time and utilizes symmetry and comfortable furniture. Originated in European culture, it includes lots of dark wood with curved and ornate details.

Transitional:

Classic traditional styling mixed with modern touches; adding modern touches such as wall art and accessories is a great way to create a transitional look. Curved, cushy ornate furniture accented with sleek details and accessories like metal, mirror, or glass is popular. Transitional furniture, for example; a sofa may have sleek, straight lines for its overall shape, but include traditional elements like a back cushion that is tufted with fuller more plush seat cushions than an all-modern sofa.

Modern:

Modern is identified by actual style elements that were popular in the U.S. around 1925-1975. There was an artistic 'movement' called modernism, highlighting clean lines, sleek surfaces, and neutral color palettes along with materials such as steel, glass, and metals. The movement transitioned from the ornate 'Hollywood Glam' era to the simpler, more organic features of 'Mid-Century Modern' (think of the Brady Bunch house). Art Deco falls within this design era as well.

Contemporary:

Although contemporary and modern are used interchangeably, contemporary styling lends itself to what is 'in style' and popular at the moment. It's very fluid and changes to fit the current trends. What's contemporary today may be different seven years from now.

Shabby Chic:

This style became popular in the 80's highlighting furniture that has history and antique qualities. Painted and distressed techniques are used on old furniture pieces. The style can be described as cozy, cottage, and vintage with materials such as soft cottons, sheers, lace, and floral.

Industrial:

Industrial is just as it sounds, utilizing items you may find in a warehouse or urban loft. Commercial tools can be transformed to create unique, one-of-a-kind furnishings. Some items that come to mind for this style are metal pipes, shiny bolts, natural wood, exposed brick on the walls, or exposed air ducts in the ceiling.

Country:

Simple, organic materials come to mind to create a country style. Wood, cotton, linen, flannels, along with lots of texture and prints like checks, plaids, and floral. It's a simple, natural style that evokes cozy, comfortable, simple living.

Farm House:

Utilizes the same elements in country styling, highlighting elements of life on the farm. Natural organic materials, soft colors of white, cream, and neutral versions of blues and grays. Of course, denim and other colors like red are popular. It has worn distressed furniture with lots of character and history.

Eclectic:

Whatever you feel goes! If you like many different styles, this may be the one for you. Eclectic styling is a blend of many styles together. Although most overall room designs include one or two elements from different styles, authentic, eclectic design is not haphazard but very intentional. Because you are blending different styles, to avoid chaos, the result must eventually be cohesive. Take some time to research this style if you think it's for you.

There are many more standard styles that exist; however, why not be even more creative and coin your personal style. When determining your design style, try to keep the process simple. The items currently in your home, and the colors and styles you wear every day provide critical clues.

Another great idea is to look at different decorating websites like houzz.com. It's essentially a décor magazine online. You can save all the photos you like in one place. This will help you identify styles that appeal to you. There are also 'style test' available online to get you started. You are uniquely and wonderfully made; your home should reflect that fact.

After learning some of the standard styles and doing your research, you may decide your style is **'Transitional.'** In my decorating business, I've found that most clients prefer 'Transitional.' It's a perfect blend of classic elements with modern accents.

If 'Transitional' is the style of choice, a cohesive design should flow from one room to another. It is important to incorporate enough 'Transitional' elements in the furniture and accessories used.

In the industry, we call this 'Harmony and Flow.' This is the process of repeating specific elements of your selected style throughout a space or the entire home. This can include colors, patterns, or even a specific shape to be repeated several times in one space and then weaved throughout the home into different rooms. This creates that connection or 'harmony and flow' which the eye seeks for a cohesive look and feel. It also helps to generate the "Wow Factor" we all desire.

Contentment

There is something very important I would like to discuss here. Be very careful about the desire to create rooms exactly as you may see them in magazines or having what you think others may 'expect' to see in your home. We can sometimes fall into that slippery slope of 'not enough' and 'what will *they* think?' Keep in mind; the magazine photos are 'staged' for the photo and not always indicative of real-life, everyday living. It's okay to use these resources as a guide, not a command.

It's essential you become very comfortable within the skin and the home you're in. Yes, I said skin. As we've learned earlier in this book, you are important to God. What you have been given is what's within you in addition to what's within your home. It should all be cherished with a grateful heart.

I Timothy 6:6 (NKJV)

"Now godliness with contentment is great gain."

Understand that being content is not being complacent. It's fine to plan for greater things, but to do so while ignoring the current things is not what God desires for you. We should never degrade what He's already provided. He is watching to see what we do with it. More to come on this topic in chapter 5.

<u>Our Design Plan</u>

Step 1 Room-	Family Room
Step 2 Design Style-	Transitional

✓ <u>Step 2 Interior Joy Check – Style</u>

1. God designed you as one-of-a-kind. Name two of your unique qualities.

2. How can you use these qualities to honor God?

3. Research a few design styles online to discover what you like best. Use the researched information as a guide to help you coin your style. What style is best for you? Use this style for the room selected in Step 1.

Step 3

Mood

God's Principle

STEP 3

ATTITUDE

Of all the things God desires for you – The right attitude is so important. As a matter of fact, with the right attitude, you just may make…the right decisions.

Your attitude is a by-product of the experiences of your mind, will, and emotions. It colors the lens through which you see the world and determines how you navigate through life. It's the soul of your existence. God cares about something so essential. And, if it's that important, guess who else wants a piece – the enemy. Your soul's attitude will either open, shut, or leave a crack to the door of worldly beliefs. Don't be fooled by the enemy. He has absolutely nothing to benefit you. God has so much waiting on you and for you. How's your attitude? Does it reside in the Spirit of God's truth or lean towards the world's view?

'You were created with the mind of Christ. You are to think like Christ, not like the world.'

I Corinthians 2:12-14, 16 (NKJV)

"Now we have received, not the spirit of the world, but the Spirit who is from God, that we might know the things that have been freely given to us by God. These things we also speak, not in words which man's wisdom teaches but which the Holy Spirit teaches, comparing spiritual things with spiritual. But the natural man does not receive the things of the Spirit of God, 'for they are foolishness to him' nor can he know them, because they are spiritually discerned. For 'who has known

the mind of the Lord that he may instruct Him?' But we have the mind of Christ."

Interior Joy is connecting to the mind and attitude of Christ. Another great example of the importance of attitude is seen in the parable of the talents. Parables are illustrations that share a religious principle or lesson.

This parable is so important that I must include it in its entirety so that you may grasp every word. It's straight from Jesus himself, as indicated by the red writing in your bible.

Matthew 25:14-30 (NKJV)

"For the kingdom of heaven is like a man traveling to a far country, who called his own servants and delivered his goods to them. And to one he gave five talents, to another two, and to another one, to each according to his own ability; and immediately he went on a journey. Then he who had received the five talents went and traded with them, and made another five talents. And likewise, he who had received two gained two more also. But he who had received one went and dug in the ground and hid his lord's money. After a long time, the lord of those servants came and settled accounts with them. So he who had received five talents came and brought five other talents, saying, 'Lord, you delivered to me five talents; look, I have gained five more talents besides them. His lord said to him, 'Well done, good and faithful servant; you were faithful over a few things, I will make you ruler over many things. Enter into the joy of your lord. He also who had received two talents came and said, lord, you delivered to me two talents; look, I have gained two more talents besides them.' His lord said to him, 'Well done, good and faithful servant; you have been faithful over a few things, I will make you ruler over many things. Enter into the joy of your lord. 'Then he who had received the one talent came and said, 'Lord, I know you to be

a hard man, reaping where you have not sown, and gathering where you have not scattered seed. 'And I was afraid, and went and hid your talent in the ground. Look, there you have what is yours. 'But his lord answered and said to him, You wicked and lazy servant, you knew that I reap where I have not sown, and gather where I have not scattered seed. 'So you ought to have deposited my money with the bankers, and at my coming, I would have received back my own with interest. 'So take the talent from him, and give it to him who has ten talents.' For everyone who has, more will be given, and he will have abundance; but from him who does not have, even what he has will be taken away. 'And cast the unprofitable servant into the outer darkness. There will be weeping and gnashing of teeth.'"

My goodness!! I'm not sure you can get any more serious than that! Did you see that ATTITUDE? When reading this parable, it may seem on the surface, that it's just about money. However, the results from each servant were predicated upon the attitude of each servant, not the quantity of talents (in this case money) received. The attitude that each servant had *before* receiving money from their lord determined their action. The attitude also helped to shape their ability. The parable clearly states their lord entrusted to each servant according to their ability.

Matthew 25:15 (NKJV)

"And to one he gave five talents, to another two, and to another one, to each according to his own ability."

We must not be so quick to blame God when we feel we do not have enough. Maybe that feeling is a bad attitude keeping us from what He intends for us to have.

It's so interesting how we can lose sight of what's in our hands and even insult God by asking 'why'... Lord, why don't I have more?

Why am I not getting the promotion, or the larger house, or the breaks I see others getting?

The servant insulted his lord by stating "Lord, I know you to be a hard man, reaping where you have not sown, and gathering where you have not scattered seed." 'Insinuating he's a difficult man expecting something from nothing.' What an insult! And this was said to the person that freely gave the servant the one talent! He received just one talent when the others received more because he couldn't handle more. He received-according to his ability. The servant demonstrated his lack of ability with his ungrateful heart and bad attitude, doing absolutely nothing with the one talent he did receive!

Talents

In life, talents can pertain to anything of value (money, gifts, abilities, resources).

If you live to experience life, for any number of years past childhood, you should not leave this earth with your talents in the same condition since birth!

The talents are being entrusted to you, that means you are being trusted to do something with it, there is an expectation that something bigger, better, greater will become of it. It is to be used, enhanced, and multiplied. It's not just for you; there is a greater purpose.

Remember…Our greater purpose is to honor God. When we honor God, many are blessed!

Don't have the attitude of the servant with one talent. This servant proved to be unprofitable; wasting what was entrusted to him and eventually thrown into outer darkness.

It's so important not to waste your talents. I'm 100% positive we can all have a better attitude than the 'one-talent' servant, how about you?

Step 3

Mood

Décor Principle

STEP 3

DÉCOR HOME MOOD

Step 3 of your home's décor plan is to determine the Mood you would like to create. What attitude would you like for your home to portray? Hmmm…gratitude perhaps?

Yes, as we've learned, gratitude is critical, and it can be used to help us translate a specific mood within the atmosphere of our homes.

You know the feeling you get when you walk into a model home? That feeling is the mood created right from the front door. Whether it's a cozy, welcoming atmosphere filled with warm tropical colors or an energetic jolt of excitement from a large beautiful wall canvas in the foyer, there's always something that sets the stage for the mood of the remaining parts of the home.

At this point in the plan, we are trying to identify the 'design mood,' not a temporary mood created for a party or some event, but a mood created from the actual design elements in the home. Colors, patterns, textures, scale, proportion, or architectural elements help to define the mood.

Is the space bright and airy or full of rich, dark hues? Is there a fireplace with floor to ceiling river stones or a room full of wallpaper with crushed crystals glistening in the pattern? These elements are not only a part of the décor style, but they generate a mood that helps to describe the space.

Many of today's homes have open floor plans where one room will seamlessly flow into the next. Each room may resemble an identical mood through the use of similar colors, patterns, or even shapes.

Let's take a look at these two spaces. The living room flows into the dining space. I would say the mood is a relaxed, casually elegant feel, while the actual décor style is 'Transitional.'

As mentioned before, it is so important to understand; it's not necessary to have our homes compete with the professional model homes out there. However, we can take a few pointers to enhance our own. The very same elements used in high-end designs can be affordably replicated in any living space.

Joyful living is creating honest spaces full of the things we love. Maybe it's a sentimental piece from a loved one or an heirloom passed down from generation to generation. These are the things that make a house a home and are certainly more important than the appearance of a perfectly staged home. Living in an unauthentic house with only 'staged' items does not create nourishing spaces of interior joy.

I am a firm believer that everyone deserves to live in a beautiful space. Whether you reside in a room that's rented or a home that's owned, your space can be a haven of love and comfort. It's all about the energy you put into it, both the spiritual and physical energy.

As stated, your attitude will determine the essence of your life's experiences. Starting with the right mindset of putting God first and having a spirit of gratitude will open the door to a creative flow that will surprise you.

So, back to the original question…what is the mood you would like to set in your space?

- *Exciting and fun?*
- *Relaxed and calm?*
- *Romantically elegant?*
- *Or Youthfully active?*

There are no hard rules, just let your needs define it?

Let's take a look at each one of the moods listed and use it for a Family Room:

Exciting and Fun

This mood sounds like we need very durable furniture that's easy to clean. The colors should evoke excitement; red, orange, and maybe yellows can fit the bill. Now, these colors do not need to be on all the walls, but they can be incorporated into the space in various ways.

There is a psychology to color that must be considered. When you think of a room being exciting, the color red may come to mind instead of white or blue. That's because there is a mood to it. Have you ever gone to a doctor's office (not a pediatrician) and seen red walls in the exam room? Most likely not. That's because the medical industry knows there's a psychology to color, and the mood of the space should support the activity. Most exam rooms are white because it's indicative of cleanliness and purity. For home, an all-white room will need to be carefully planned to incorporate a lot of texture and maybe various degrees of white. Otherwise, it will be too stark and fall flat.

We will get more in-depth on the topic of color in the next chapter.

Relaxed and Calm

This mood may create images of sofas with large cozy cushions, lots of pillows, and neutral wall colors. There may be limited numbers of accessories to reduce clutter, or there may be an abundance of items to help create a feeling of security and familiarity – family photos, favorite books, candles, etc. All dependent upon your taste and needs.

Romantically Elegant

This mood conjures images of soft colors like sky blue and ivory whites with patterns that are traditional with soft prints like damasks or even floral. French and even shabby chic designs may be the way to go. Now, any design style (Traditional, Country, and even Modern) can be maneuvered to create a romantically elegant mood. Remember, the mood is not the design style; it is the feeling you want to have when you're in the space.

Youthfully Active

This mood sounds like a space for children. They can be toddlers or teenagers. I can envision inexpensive modular furniture that's easy to move around, a ping-pong table, or some sort of activity table for games and toys if the children are younger. The color scheme could include various colors, or the main wall surfaces can be neutral while fun video chairs and toys add a pop of color.

There are a million ways to create your dream!

<u>Our Design Plan</u>

Step 1	Room-	Family Room
Step 2	Style-	Transitional
Step 3	**Mood-**	Casual Elegance

✓ Step 3 Interior Joy Check – Mood

1. What is your attitude about your home?

2. What adjustment can you make to your attitude to show more gratitude?

3. The room you selected in step 1, what is the mood you would like to achieve?

Step 4

Color Scheme
God's Principle

STEP 4

STRATEGIC INTENTIONS

Strategy, that's what we need, whether in life or enhancing our home's atmosphere.

Envision with me a 'life dream'; all major milestones have been strategically planned and achieved by the dreamer.

Age 25- homeownership, 35- married (maybe 4 kids), 40- business ownership, age 45- multiple millions made and saved, 55- financially independent and traveling the world, age 65- birds are the alarm clock, in excellent health and now mentoring others on how to achieve the same.

Wow!... sounds like an awesome 'life dream' of worthy achievements to me! The strategy had to be solid!

If this 'life dream' does not describe your life, don't be dismayed. If it does, please be my mentor!

Now… As I awake from the dream, I realize, even with all my strategizing and planning, God orders the steps and has the final say.

Proverbs 16:9 (NKJV)

"A man's heart plans his way, but the Lord directs his steps."

Proverbs 19:21 (NKJV)

"There are many plans in a man's heart, nevertheless the Lord's counsel---that will stand."

No, life is not perfect. In our planning, we must be open to God's direction. We may plan to go left, but God may redirect to the right.

The ability to dream in the first place is because He created us in His image… to think, plan and envision our future; it's all because of God's intention.

- God's strategy is in His steps.
- Steps denote a process.
- A process takes time.
- Time allows for lessons learned.

Anything worth achieving will have many detours and lessons along the way.

There's no need to get upset when things don't look exactly as you planned. Stay on track and learn the lessons. Have intention, keep planning, but be open to God's version of those plans. He has great plans for you.

Jeremiah 29:11 (NKJV)

"For I know the thoughts that I think toward you, says the Lord, thoughts of peace and not of evil, to give you a future and a hope."

Our best plans sometimes fail, but this is not the prescription for giving up, it is the ingredient for getting up and asking what's next? What's the next step, Lord?

If you are wondering what steps to take today and you are unsure, don't worry. What is the last step God gave you? What do you have to work with right now? Make sure that it is fully complete before looking for a new one. He will never leave you guessing.

Be assured that no matter what lies before you, God intends to work it all out, good and bad to his divine, strategic order!

Romans 8:28 (NKJV)

"And we know that all things work together for good to those who love God, to those who are the called according to His purpose."

Be intentional, have a strategy, but leave room for God!

Step 4

Color Scheme

Décor Principle

STEP 4

DÉCOR COLOR SCHEME

Just as God is strategic and orders the steps to our life, we must be strategic in determining our home's color scheme.

A strategy is needed for your home's color scheme to achieve the best results.

This step can be challenging to some, especially when the home has an open floor-plan where several rooms can be viewed from one location. I hear it all the time from clients, "I'm not sure where to stop one color and begin a new one', "I have to be sure all the colors blend and complement one another."

Although this step can be challenging at times, it's one of the most enjoyable. Color is interesting, and there is a psychology to color. It has an effect on the attitude and mood of your space.

There isn't a lot of scientific data proving the mood effects of color, but sometimes pure life experience will provide enough 'real-world' data to prove the effects. Cultural influences, life experiences, and personal preferences all play a role in how color affects one's mood.

It is well noted that the color white can have an opposing effect depending on the cultural influence. In Western countries, it is seen as a symbol of purity, cleanliness, and innocence, however, in Eastern countries, it represents mourning.

In your own life, a specific color can ignite a happy or sad moment. Maybe you had a traumatic experience in a car, for instance, that happened to be blue. Possibly, this can conjure an uncomfortable memory and, therefore, a feeling or mood you would prefer to refrain from. If this is the case, you may stay away from cars in the future that are blue. It could even impact the color preferences for your clothing or home. This may seem extreme, but everyone is different, and we all have our likes and dislikes.

Overall, we have a personal response to color. Color is very subjective; however, there are general concepts (depending on the culture) to the effects of color.

(Cool Tones)

✓ **Blue-**   **Relaxing, calm, dependable, sad, depression**

✓ **Green-**   **Nature, renewal, calm, organic, envy, growth**

(Warm Tones)

✓ **Red-**   **Love, excitement, energy, action, danger, bold**

✓ **Yellow-**   **Happy, confident, energy**

✓ **Orange-**   **Enthusiasm, vibrant, attention**

(Neutrals)

✓ **Black-**   **Power, sophistication, formal, mystery, strength, depression (Considered to be the absence of color)**

✓ **White-**   **Pure, clean, youthful, empty, cold, sterile, unfriendly. (Considered to be the sum of all *possible* colors.)**

✓ **Brown-**   **Reliable, strong, wholesome, earth. (Considered a composite color. A combination of yellow, red, and black.)**

(Secondary Colors neither warm nor cool)

- ✓ **Purple-** **Wealth, royal, depression.**
- ✓ **Pink-** **Romance, kindness**
- ✓ **Magenta-** **Compassion, kindness, cooperation**

If you noticed in the descriptions, the emotion evoked for some colors could represent opposite ends of the spectrum; white- (pure and unfriendly), Red- (love and danger), Black- (Power and depressed).

The definition you put to these descriptions based on your personal experiences is important. The general descriptions are to be used as a guide to provide just a little more information to the process of enhancing your environment. Remember, this is your personal space, and what you desire is what's best. Your Interior Joy is the goal!

When selecting a color, it's good to start with at least three colors to create visual depth and interest. You also must remember your floor and ceiling are two of the largest areas in the room itself. Therefore, the colors of those areas are important to the overall color scheme.

When selecting color- the 'undertones' or 'bias' of the color must be considered. This critical element can make or break the final look of your space. If you are selecting three colors to start your rooms color scheme- let's say **tan and gray with an orange accent color**, all three of these colors should have similar undertones to coordinate nicely. This is the easiest way to achieve a visually pleasing result.

Now, what do I mean by undertone? Undertones can be warm, cool, or neutral. As stated earlier, warm colors include red, orange, and yellow. Cool colors include green and blue.

How these colors relate to each other on a color wheel determines their undertone or 'bias' to one another. A color wheel is an illustration of the relationship of various colors presented in a circle or wheel formation.

Color Wheel recreation by Jasmine Holder, age 15. (See Notes 3)

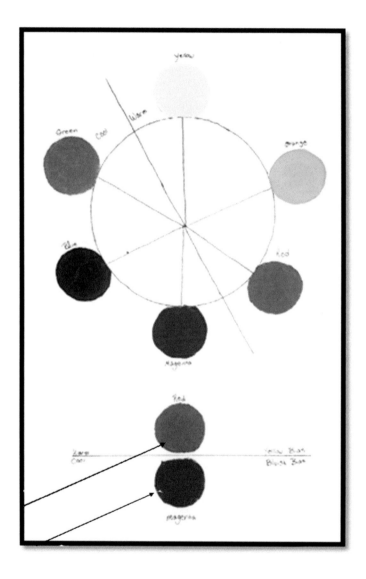

<u>Red</u> can have a yellow undertone (warm) or a bluish undertone (cool)

<u>Magenta</u> is the 'cool tone' version of red.

There are cool and warm versions of all secondary colors. Again yellow and red are warm colors, and blue and green are cool colors.

The secondary versions of these colors have a 'bias' to be either warm or cool.

Yellow   Yellowish Red   Yellowish Green

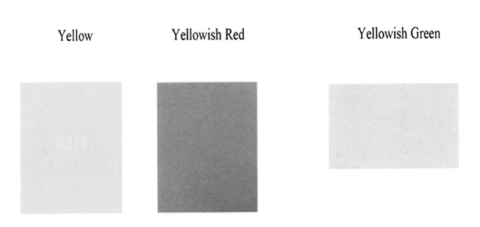

To keep it simple, the undertones (bias) will be either cool or warm. Creating a color scheme with colors of the same undertone is a simple way to ensure your colors coordinate and flow nicely from one room to the other.

To avoid getting too complicated with the color definitions of hues, shades, tones, and undertones, we will keep it simple just to highlight undertones.

The easiest way to see undertones is to view the same color side-by-side.

Take a look at three versions of gray here.

Gray #1 has a warm (yellow) undertone.

Gray #2 has a blue (cool) undertone.

Gray #3 has a purple undertone. (Purple is a secondary color that's neither warm nor cool.)

Believe it or not, each color here is gray!

#1.   #2.   #3.

Here each **column** represents the start of a color scheme- Gray, Tan, and an Accent Color.

The same colors with different undertones viewed side-by-side almost look like different hues (colors). A color scheme can certainly have more than 3 colors, but it's best to start there.

Column 1 shows a color scheme with warm undertones- for gray, tan, and accent color- orange.

Column 2 shows a color scheme with cool undertones- for gray, tan, and accent color- blue.

Column 3 shows a color scheme with purple undertones- for gray, tan, and accent color- purple.

It may take some time, but you will be able to identify the undertones with more practice now that you're aware of its effect.

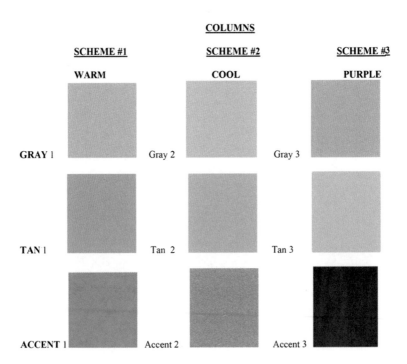

We've selected colors with the same undertone to make sure the colors coordinate well in the same room while also flowing seamlessly into the next room.

<u>Our Design Plan</u>

Step 1	Room	Family Room
Step 2	Style	Transitional
Step 3	Mood	Casual Elegance
Step 4	**Color Scheme**	Gray, Tan, Cinnamon

✓ Step 4 Interior Joy Check – Color Scheme

1. What top goal would you like to achieve in the next three years?

2. Ask God what He would like for you to work on today as part of your strategy.

3. For the room you selected in step 1, what three colors would you select to start the color scheme?

Step 5

Furniture
God's Principle

STEP 5

USE WHAT YOU HAVE

'But the look is outdated...as her eyes perused the front entry of her home. When will I ever get the money to get rid of this old wallpaper? The kitchen cabinets are old, the window treatments in the living room are outdated, and the style is something I would never pick today. How did this happen? Sixteen years have passed and no change to the décor? Sigh... This space certainly does not represent me today, not even a little bit!'

Portions of this scenario were shared earlier in the book. You may relate to one or two elements yourself. As a professional decorator, I've seen hundreds of homes; no two homes are alike. Most times, I get the stress call from the woman of the house; however, sometimes the husband recommends to the wife, "Please give a decorator a call."

Whether you're married, single, or have roommates, the care of the home is usually 'taken-on' by the woman of the house. In typical situations, the intention is to maintain a comfortable, clean, organized space, but reality takes hold, and life gets in the way.

For me, decorating as a profession increases the importance of my home's atmosphere. It's more than just décor; it represents my talent as a professional. There's nothing worse than avoiding company because of the displeasure of my own home. I didn't like that it projected an image of past decades and 'yester-year' style. I no longer desired the Roman neoclassical embellishments that adorned my windows, furniture, and walls. I now looked at the furniture in despair wondering, 'how could I ever have an interest in a side table with carved images of people in togas? What in the world was

I thinking?' But here it was- 16 years later, and these items were still in my home. No change.

Now you may say, okay Charisse, you are a professional decorator, if it was that bad, why didn't you change it? Well, ...life, babies, building a business, and other priorities, just to name a few, required the most attention. Maybe some of this sounds familiar to your life story. We all have our lives to live and important things to do; sometimes, our homes are put on the back of the back-burners. It's just not that easy sometimes.

Remember step 3- attitude and the talents? I needed an attitude shift and to ...

Use what I *had* to the fullest.

Matthew 25:21 (NKJV)

"...Well done, good and faithful servant, you were faithful over a few things, I will make you ruler over many things."

At a minimum, it's necessary to clean our homes on a regular basis and de-clutter when possible. After this, comes the decorating. Now, decorating may not be a life-or-death situation, but it certainly enhances living. Your home's atmosphere matters!

When you feel it's time to enhance your decor, ask yourself this important question, it will determine if decorating is viable at this time. It will also reveal whether you've maximized your skills and abilities. I've titled this question the 'Litmus Test' question. This will help you reposition your attitude and remove any guilt, shame, or discontent about the current state of your space.

Ask yourself...

'Is there more I can do, to maximize what I have, within my ability, in this season of my life?'

I love this question because it creates a realistic perspective and helps to determine if decorating is possible- right now. It will also determine if you're 'using what you have' to the max.

When you answer 'yes' to this question- there's more you can do. Either something can be re-purposed, painted, upholstered, or maybe purchased.

A 'no' answer says-all has been done, for now. Your ability, skills, finances, and or time have been maximized. If your honest answer is no, please don't beat yourself up. Take a deep breath, sit in the seat of your situation, and be grateful for what you have. Now is the time to focus on other priorities and look forward to changes later. Be content and experience the 'interior joy' God has purposed for you-now.

By asking this question, it helps you to see where you are at the moment. It will either reveal an answer that moves you forward towards making the changes-now; or help you to be patient with an 'attitude shift' to do something later.

If the answer is yes, let's revisit that scenario, with the lens of a new attitude to maximize what we have.

New Attitude

Okay …I know the wallpaper is old, the neoclassical 'toga-wearing' people on the side tables are outdated, and my kitchen cabinets need updating, but what can I do right now? I am in a position to do something, but what? Can I remove the old wallpaper and paint myself? Can I take down the old window treatments and let the beauty of the window molding take center stage? Can I replace the toga side tables with two nightstands refurbished from the guest room? How about painting- instead of replacing my old kitchen cabinets? YES, I CAN!!! I am grateful for what I have, and now excited about what I can do.'

With an attitude shift, gratitude emerges, and creativity increases.

Attitude → Gratitude → Creativity

The new attitude allows for a more creative outlook. The lens becomes clearer, and the mind can envision new uses for old things. This is the moment we tap into the 'interior joy' that's already present.

Maximize what you have.

Are you fully using all that you have? Are there unused furnishings around your house? Is there something that can be re-purposed and used differently? Any items in the garage waiting to be re-discovered?

According to my ability?

Do you have a special talent like sewing, painting, arts and crafts, or building? Maybe you enjoy flea market up-cycling.

In this season of my life?

Now, this is the clincher. This is the portion of the question that truly determines if you're in a position to decorate or make changes to your space. See, although you may be crafty and there are items you would love to get your hands on- to sand, paint, and make it spectacular; it may not be your season to do so. Is your time completely used by the care of a new baby? How are the funds currently? Even if you (DIY) do it yourself, that may require some funds.

Sometimes, things are on hold until God says, now is the time! When He says move, you must move. There's no time for procrastination when the window of opportunity presents itself. When God says 'move' and you are positioned under His window of opportunity, don't snooze, you've got to move. Things change on a daily basis, and the window may close!

Contentment

Understand, being content does not mean being complacent. They have two different meanings entirely. Contentment says, "Yes, Lord, I appreciate all that I have, and I will maximize it to the best of my ability. I'm grateful right here, right now, until you say move!" There is no more I can do at this time.

Being complacent is not a spirit of gratitude; instead, it's a spirit of laziness. Having no desire to change what needs to be improved, is the opposite of contentment.

The lesson here is:

1. Maximize what's been entrusted to you
2. Be content
3. Move when God says move.

Step 5

Furniture

Décor Principle

STEP 5

DÉCOR FURNITURE

Now, It's time to 'Use what you have' to maximize what you already own. Here is where you determine which furniture pieces will be re-purposed or purchased new for your room design.

Up to this point, you have:

- ✓ **1. Started with a plan for your room and its function.**
- ✓ **2. Identified your design style.**
- ✓ **3. Determined the mood for the space.**
- ✓ **4. Selected a color scheme.**
- ✓ **5. Now it's time to select your furniture.**

The furniture to support our activities planned is listed below.

Our Design Plan

Step 1 - Room & Function	Family Room. Relaxed, casual fun TV viewing, Napping, Games, Reading, homework. Everyday users- Two adults. Two kids. No pets.
Step 2 - Style-	Transitional
Step 3 - Mood-	Casual Elegance
Step 4 - Color Scheme-	Gray, Tan, Cinnamon
Step 5 - Furniture-	Sectional Sofa, Recliner, Coffee Table, End Tables, Sofa Table, Desk, Game Table with chairs, Accent Chairs with table, Rug, Bookcase, Lamps.

In my own home as an example, I had a table and a set of chairs that I owned for 21 years. I know that's a long time, so I'm sure you understand that I was more than ready for a replacement.

However, remembering that very important question we must ask ourselves before decorating any space…

"Can I do more to maximize what I have, according to my ability, in this season of my life?"

My answer was 'yes" to the total question. Since my answer was yes, this indicated there was more I could do with what I had. I needed to have an attitude of gratitude and get creative to extend the use of this table even longer.

Again, the 'clincher' that's important in this question is 'what season of your life are you currently in?' Although I got great use out of the table and chairs over the last 23 years, in my current season, finances required that I do more with the table set before purchasing a new one. There were too many other financial priorities that required my immediate attention.

So my 'total' answer is 'Yes, I can do more.'

Each individual will have a different reason for their answer. For one, it may be financial, for other finances are good, but time and priority are not amenable. Maybe you have a brand new set of twins just born. Everyone has a personal reason for their answer.

For me, the desire for 'new' outweighed the cash available. I was also in a place of decreasing debt, so using credit was not an option.

After I got over the fact that I was not getting a new dining set, I took a deep breath, prayed, and expressed my gratitude for what I already owned. I then asked myself, "What can I do to enhance this table and these chairs?" I took some time to sit and ponder.

Maybe I can do something with the base of the table?

The table had a 60" rectangle glass top with a large ceramic pedestal base. The base was a natural ivory color with a small amount of antique stain on the surface.

Now, as I explained earlier in the book, I had no interest in keeping the neoclassical style of the former design of my home. Just as I wondered how I could ever purchase living room side tables with toga-wearing people carved on the front, I had the same attitude with the fleur-de-lis styled table base.

Beautiful… but beautifully outdated. (For me.)

To "use what I had to creatively get what I wanted," I knew I had to quickly change my attitude, remove that thought and figure something out.

So, the first creative idea to emerge was to order new chair covers. Now, that may not sound creative to you, but the thought began to "awaken joy"! Even though the chairs already had covers used for the past 16 years, they did not match the new color scheme. I made the current covers back in 2002 and remembered how long it took me, so making new ones was out of the question. I just did not have the time.

Sometimes, 'according to your ability' means replacing with something inexpensive. Since the budget was low, it was important for me to find something at a reasonable price.

Then another thought came, "Why don't I paint the ceramic base?" I have paint from past projects and decided to give it a try. The results were great. Not necessarily what I would purchase in the store today, but better than the plain white base I had. In this case, I loved it!!

Now, remember, your home should represent what you like. Please, no comparisons or desires for what others may think or have. Maintain a spirit of gratitude for what you already own.

After painting the base, I decided to paint the legs of the chairs. The chairs were parson chairs, but every part of the chair was covered in fabric, including the legs.

The new chair cover stopped just below the seat and left the legs exposed. This was not going to work, so I decided to use fabric paint and paint the legs black. I stepped back and took a look… Hmmm, not bad.

BEFORE   **AFTER**

The ideas continued to flow. I found a new fabric to create some very simple window treatments and decided to use a small amount of the same fabric on the chairs. I considered different ways to use the fabric.

In the end, I decided to create what I call a 'chair topper' on the seatback of the chair and use the same fabric to create a fabric band around the base of the chair cover. The ideas continued to flow, and I added a jeweled pendant as a tassel on the back of each newly created chair topper.

Okay, Lord, I like it! It's different, it complements the style I was going for, and it truly transformed the room.

The creativity continued, and I decided to make a unique and 'quirky' centerpiece for the table. I saw a very unique and organic centerpiece at a high-end restaurant. It inspired me to create one of my own. Its one-of-a-kind and I love it!

The beautiful vase is an item I selected from an event held by my church 'First Baptist Church of Glenarden.' The church held a Women's Conference and included a 'Free Market' full of wonderful donated items to bless anyone who had an interest. God is always in the blessing business! This may not be for everybody, but it sure works for me!

BEFORE

BEFORE

See the Toga wearing people?

AFTER

AFTER
This maximizing thing is great! I loved the results!
Gratitude = Creativity

Furniture Fit

One of the most important factors in selecting furniture is making sure it fits! You must measure the full room and the area for each piece of furniture. Furniture size can be deceiving in the large furniture stores. A piece that's too big will appear 'normal size' in a warehouse, but it's most likely too large for a room in your home.

Scale and Proportion

The scale and proportion of furniture and accessories play a vital role in the final look of your design.

Scale refers to the size of an item compared to its surrounding space.

Proportion is the size of one object compared to another object.

Balance between elements, color, texture, and shapes must be achieved.

Let's take a look at our room from earlier. As beautiful as this sofa is (View #1), the scale and proportion are all wrong! The style is great, but the size is not. This mistake happens way too often. Clients fall in love with an item and purchase without understanding this design principle.

The scale is too small for the space, and the proportion is too small with the surrounding items (side tables, coffee table, and accessories). This can be frustrating when you invest a lot of money into something you really like, and you can't figure out why the look and feel of the space are off.

VIEW #1

The next sofa (View #2) it is better in scale and proportion to the space and the objects around it. The end tables are still a little over-scaled, but I do enjoy using slightly larger-scaled items now and then, as long as it still works visually. Remember, it's your space, and these are guidelines to assist you. It's not about being perfect; however, having a strategy and plan will keep you from making costly mistakes.

VIEW #2

Now let's take a look at the lamps on the end tables of the same living room. The lamp and accessories on the left are better in scale and proportion than the lamp and accessory group on the right.

The scale of the lamp on the left is good. The lamp base and shade are the proper scale to the space surrounding it. The proportion is good compared to the objects around it (sofa, table, and accessories).

The lamp on the right has a base and shade that's too skinny in scale compared to the surrounding space. The proportion of the lamp is too small compared to the other objects around it (sofa and end table it's sitting on).

The lamps are a part of our lighting plan. They are the 'task' lighting, so; it's important to be sure they are tall enough for the task of reading, for instance.

In general, when purchasing furniture or accessories, always consider the size of the space and items surrounding it. Don't make a purchase just because you like the style. It needs to meet all the requirements of your full design plan.

In the end, it's your preference; however, these design principles are an important guide to help you achieve your dream without wasting time and money!

To ensure a proper fit, it's a great idea to draw the shape of your space onto graph paper. You don't have to get too technical. Even a basic shape like the length and width of the room can get you started. Each square on the graph paper represents 1 foot or 12 inches.

When you determine your layout, which we will cover in the next chapter, you will measure the space selected for each piece of furniture. Make sure when you go shopping, you only select pieces that fit the measurement of the space. For instance, if the wall for a bench, I would like to purchase is 103" (inches) I will make sure my bench is less than 60". I may decide I would like to have at least 20" of open wall space on each side of the bench.

Here is a portion of a rough sketch for a basement space from one of my consultations.

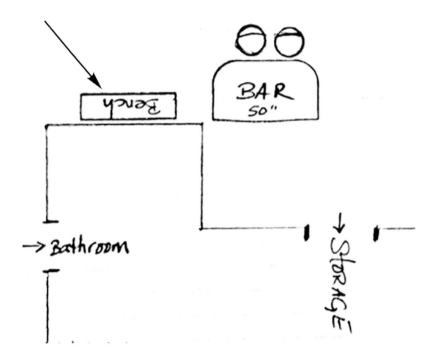

<u>Core Pieces</u>

Your core furniture pieces are the pieces that anchor the room. They are usually the 'workhorse' items getting most of the use. For instance, in a living room, the sofa is typically used most, in a bedroom; the bed, in the dining room, of course, the dining table and chairs are the core pieces.

The function of the space naturally determines the layout of the core pieces. In a family room, if TV viewing is the main activity, placing the sofa in front of the wall with the TV works best. And now, that 'TV wall' is a focal point. If there will be no TV viewing, the sofa may be placed across from a large window with a view or a sliding door. That 'window wall' now becomes a focal point. The focal wall is a great place to add an accent color or unique wall hanging.

New Purpose

In addition to refreshing items you currently own, you can re-purpose items from other rooms and give them a new purpose in a different space.

- ✓ **A bedroom dresser used as a dining room sideboard. (View #3)**
- ✓ **A bedroom nightstand used as a console in the foyer. (View #4)**
- ✓ **A short bookcase used to define a foyer entry. (View #5)**
- ✓ **Two tall bookcases placed back-to-back serving both as a room divider for a headboard and a beautiful closet simultaneously. (View #6 and #7)**

VIEW #3

VIEW #4

VIEW #5

VIEW #6

VIEW #7

With our new mindset of gratitude and creativity, the sky is the limit. When we understand this truth, we will see that God is the true provider. The only way to living our God-designed life of Interior Joy.

"Well done good and faithful servant... enter into the joy of your master!"

✓ Step 5 Interior Joy Check – Furniture

1. What's your answer to the "Litmus Test' question for the space you selected in step 1?

2. What items can you maximize and re-purpose for your space?

3. At this point in the book, what has awakened interior joy for you thus far?

Step 6

Layout

God's Principle

STEP 6

ORDER

I Corinthians 14:40

Let all things be done decently and in order.

There are many who struggle with what's called-'stinkin-thinkin.' I've heard this term used many times by various speakers. It's the negative stories and lies we tell ourselves for various reasons. Even with joy onboard, we encounter those moments and times in our lives when things just aren't going quite right.

Now, what does this have to do with order? Let's take a closer look.

Matthew 12:43 is so helpful in highlighting the truth of how the enemy works.

Removing bad thoughts and trying to think positive is not enough to get rid of 'stinkin-thinkin.' That is a myth many of us have fallen prey to, at one time or another. The truth of the matter is that's only a portion of the process. God said, *"Let all things be done decently and in order."* **I Corinthians 14:40 (NKJV)**

Let's take a look at the parable of the 'unclean spirit'

Matthew 12:43 (NKJV)

"When an unclean spirit goes out of a man, he goes through dry places, seeking rest, and finds none. Then he says, 'I will return to my house from which I came.' And when he comes, he finds it empty, swept, and put in order. Then he goes and

takes with him seven other spirits more wicked than himself, and they enter and dwell there, and; the last state of that man is worse than the first. So shall it also be with this wicked generation."

There are many lessons to take from this parable, but I am going to focus on the empty spaces and the interesting order of what took place.

The unclean spirit left, it no longer remained, leaving the space empty!

After leaving the man, the unclean spirit went through dry places to find a new location but instead returned to the house (the 'empty' space).

This concept applies to our minds and our homes. Stay with me; I promise we are going somewhere.

Imagine there's one room in your home in need of de-cluttering. It's that place that's lost its purpose and now houses the displaced items of your life.

For this example, the space can be the home office.

Years ago, you put the time into getting the office set up. There's a desk, chair, and all the necessary tools for business. It started as a wonderful place to think and work. You were so productive, and all was going well.

However, somehow over time, it morphed into a space you no longer spent quality, working time. You noticed the once clean corners now serving as extra storage space for books, magazines, and old binders. The desk no longer serves its purpose due to the many papers and junk mail from previous months. The free-standing bookcase has turned into an all-purpose shelf of pictures and old business venture materials. Over the years, the room has turned into something you no longer recognize.

You begin to own the fact that something needs to be done. The clutter must be removed before you can even think of sitting in that space again. However, weeks turn into months and months into years. Every time you pass the space, you just shake your head, saying to yourself, "How did this space get like this? How can one person own so much stuff? Where do I even begin?"

A few more months pass by, and you finally decide to do something about it, to tackle the junk head-on. Not only are you going to tackle the junk, you are going to decorate the space with all new furniture and accessories; a new desk, chair, bookshelf, file cabinet, wall-art, the works.

The vision of your new space brings a new sense of excitement. You begin to write a plan, determine the style, mood, color scheme, furniture, layout, lighting, and accessories – a full plan. But first, you decide to empty the space to get a clean start.

One weekend, you roll up your sleeves and get to work. You spend the entire week removing everything from the space. Books, papers, folders, magazines, that rusted old file cabinet, outdated computers, boxes, clothes (yes clothes), everything!

Late night, after a full week, you sit down exhausted in the middle of the room, so proud of all your hard work. You are so elated; you decide to enjoy the empty space just a little while longer. You feel you deserve a break after what feels like the result of running a marathon. You're sore, and aching muscles are ready for respite.

Whew... you say to yourself, now that's much better.

You enjoy the look of the empty space a little longer.

But after a while, it happens…little by little, over time, its back- in full force, total clutter. But now you have stuff from the kitchen, items removed from other rooms, and 60% of the junk you took out months earlier. Now there's significantly more junk than you had before!

You think to yourself…What happened? Why did the plan and all my hard work fail?

Empty spaces, especially those remaining empty for years, are not being maximized. We've already learned that we must 'use what we have.'

The room has now gone through extremes, clutter, and empty. Neither of these scenarios are properly maximizing the space.

You find yourself depressed again. Not only is the office cluttered again, your mind is doing the same. Cluttered with the negative thoughts from before, and even more.

Now, before we go on, in the verse, it's also interesting to note this point:

Matthew 12:44 (NKJV)

"...he finds it empty, swept, and put in order."

How can something be empty and put in order? What's in order if it's empty?

I had to sit and ponder that for a moment.

Just because something is empty, doesn't mean it's now better or 'in order.'

How many times have we tried to forget something, just get it out of our minds and try to think positive? I know I've done it many times but, to no avail. The 'stinkin- thinkin' just returns, sometimes worse than before. Why is this?

The Empty space and mind caused the enemy to return!

Not just return himself, he brought lots of enemy friends with him! Friends whose spirits were even worse. In addition, there's more space to hold a greater number of evil spirits.

Wow! Empty = Enemy

Empty spaces will either attract physical junk into your space or emotional junk into the mind.

Not only is this not best for our minds, when rooms are left empty, for long periods, it can sometimes be an indicator of something more. Has a loved one been lost? Are we afraid of commitment? Do we feel we don't deserve a better space? Are we avoiding moving forward?

That's a deeper conversation for the experts, but I have experienced it all over the years as a professional Decorator. If any of these scenarios describe your situation, please stop here and think about it. To acknowledge it allows you the ability to start the healing process.

Now that we've established that empty is not necessarily good, the question remains, how can something empty have order? Nothing remains to put in order.

The lesson here is...empty is what the enemy needs for 'his' order.

The empty order that was created was the perfect platform for the enemy to take precedence. The space was now empty and 'in order' for the enemy to use. The space is now even larger for him to return and bring his accomplices, making matters worse than before.

Leaving empty space after removal of negative self-talk, guilt, shame, judgments, insecurities, self-sabotage, inferiority, victimizations, betrayal- is a dangerous thing.

Empty is grounds for the ***Enemy!***

When the bad is removed, it must be replaced with the good, not left empty.

About your home's space, it's best to have a plan before you empty the space. This allows you to be prepared and able to replace it with the right items in order. This will guard against the enemy of clutter returning.

There's more!

Matthew 12:43 (NKJV)

"When an unclean spirit goes out of a man, he goes through dry places, seeking rest, and finds none."

Now, the unclean spirit left the man (it was cleaned out) and went through dry places.

Why were the other places dry? Maybe they were already in the condition the enemy wanted- negative, self-sabotaging thoughts. It did not find rest there because those places were already enemy prone. They were set. There was no need for this enemy to reside there.

So what does the enemy do?

Matthew 12:43-45 (NKJV)

"Then he says, 'I will return to my house from which I came.' And when he comes, he finds it empty, swept, and put in order. Then he goes and takes with him seven other spirits more wicked than himself, and they enter and dwell there, and the last state of that man is worse than the first."

Do you know anyone who tried to do it all on their own? Determined to stop whatever was not working in their life but struggled to stay on the right path?

We try to 'self medicate' our problems. Thinking we must first fix ourselves. Unfortunately, our remedy for fixing is to try and empty the thoughts.

However, trying to forget and sweep away the wrong thoughts, acts, or whatever is the issue, is not enough. We don't need to waste time. We are fighting an enemy that's calculating and determined to destroy- at all costs. What we may think is improving on our own, is grounds for the enemy to wreak greater havoc.

We can't do it ourselves. Instead of trying to fix the problem, we need to immediately go to God. Don't waste any time! He provides the strength we need to start the orderly process of renewing our minds.

This message is two-fold:

1. God shows us there is a process, an *order*, for removing the enemy from our minds. We must first seek Him.

2. Empty is grounds for the enemy. *Empty = Enemy

*Look how close those two words resemble each other. It has the same number of letters beginning and ending with the same letter, and if you read it too fast, you may mistake it for the same word.

So what's the ORDER?

The 3 R's

- ✓ *1. Replace* **with God**
- ✓ *2. Remove* **the enemy**
- ✓ *3. Renew* **our minds with truth filling the empty space.**

There is an order to renewing your mind and your space.

When we try to remove 'stinkin'-thinkin' ourselves we are out of order! God's order is not to first remove. That's Step #2. We cast down these thoughts in Step #1, which is to replace with God, to seek first the kingdom of God (Mathew 6:33).

Step #1 takes care of Step #2 and Step #3. Negative thoughts are from the enemy; not God. So we must immediately replace with God who removes the enemy and renews the mind.

Don't give ORDER to the enemy, that hierarchy belongs to God. Let God reign and take residence. He will show you how to properly fill those spaces by spending time with Him!

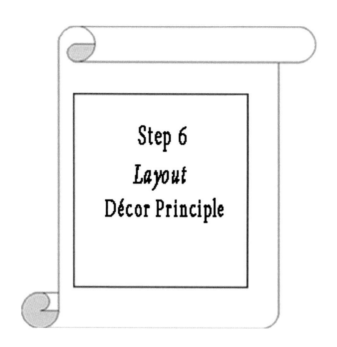

Step 6
Layout
Décor Principle

STEP 6

DÉCOR LAYOUT

Just as there is 'order' to removing the enemy from our minds and replacing it with God's truth, we must make plans for the proper order and arrangement of furnishings for our room design. This can be another challenging area for many…creating a successful 'Room Layout.'

Furniture arrangement in a room is determined by several factors:

- ✓ **Function of the space**
- ✓ **Size of the space**
- ✓ **Shape of the space**
- ✓ **Location of windows and doors**

One of the first steps in determining the furniture order in your space is to step back and get a full view. If you can empty the space, that's optimal; however, I understand this may not always be possible. The next step is to visualize the possibility of creating several 'zones' of seating for multiple functions. This is the secret to fully maximizing the use of the space, and no square footage will go to waste.

'Single zone' room layouts happen often. And typically, all the furniture is placed against the wall. When this is done, from the very beginning, you've limited the rooms function, mood, and overall design. Contrary to what many may think, placing all seating against the wall does not result in more usable space. It actually decreases the room's function, causing what I call 'long-distance' conversation seating. Arranging your furniture in this manner hampers your ability to communicate with others because they are seated too far away. If and when possible, it's best to 'float' at least one form of seating into the room, across from other seating.

Let's take a look at the Design Plan for our Family Room...

Our Design Plan

Step 1 - Room & Function	Family Room. Everyday living- Two adults. Two kids. No pets. Family get-togethers, TV viewing, Entertaining, Napping, Games, Reading and Homework.
Step 2 - Style	Transitional
Step 3 - Mood	Casual Elegance
Step 4 - Color Scheme	Warm Gray, Tan, White, Cinnamon
Step 5 - Furniture	Sectional Sofa, Accent Chair, Coffee Table, End Tables, Desk, Game Table with chairs, Accent Chairs with table, Rug, Bookcase, Lamps.
Step 6 - Order/Layout	The furniture order/arrangement is determined by the function determined in Step #1

FAMILY ROOM

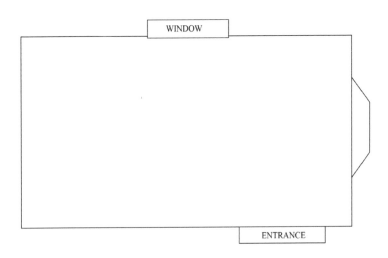

Using our floor plan created earlier, here is the room layout I see in many homes.

This is the 'one zone' room layout.

This layout shows the furniture against the walls creating the 'long-distance conversation' seating arrangement. It is difficult and uncomfortable for the person sitting in the love seat to have a conversation with the people on the sofa or person in the chair. This creates a space that is too spread apart and not very cozy or welcoming.

Outside of a better layout, what other elements in this design can be improved?

» The scale and proportion of the lamps are too small.
» The scale of the pictures and photos on the wall is too small.
» The scale of the area rug is too small.
» It needs wall color for warmth.
» It needs more lighting.

If white walls are preferred, it's important to include this option in your design plan. Without additional design elements like interesting textures and various shades of white for depth, the room style will appear flat and uninteresting.

How can this layout be improved? Let's take a look at several layout options.

LAYOUT #1

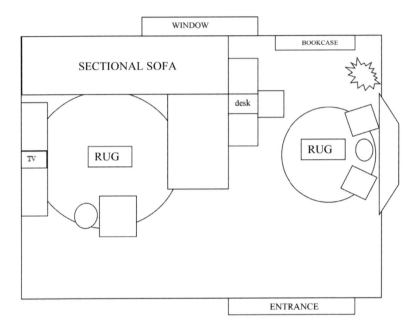

LAYOUT #2

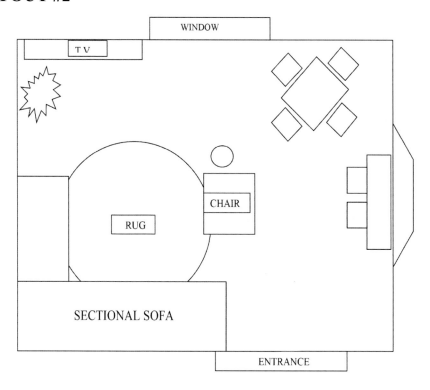

LAYOUT #3

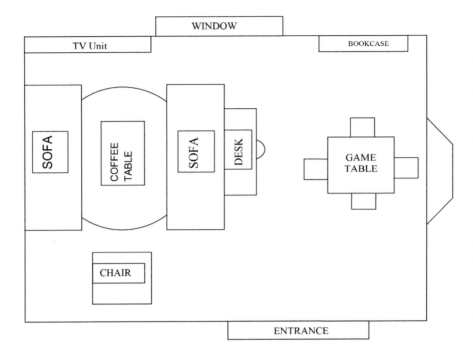

LAYOUT #4

The 'ONE ZONE' layout

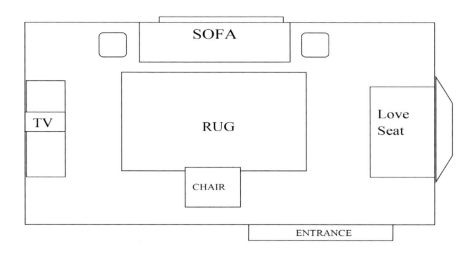

Layout #1-3 are all layout options that will seat nine people.

The number of people in your family should determine the number of seats placed in the space. I am a firm believer that a space should be decorated predominantly based on the number of family members who will use the space on a daily basis. For this family, there are a total of four family members. Having more seats is fine; however, trying to incorporate enough seats for that once a year party of 20 people when only four live there everyday is not necessary. Many times we try to decorate based on the parties we envision having, but the reality is there may be fewer parties throughout the year than we may imagine. The season of decorating is an exciting time, and we must be careful not to over-do it.

__Layout option #1__

This layout has a sectional sofa that seats five, an expandable table/desk with one chair, an accent chair for one, and a sitting area within the bay window for two; that is a total of nine seats. The sofa table/desk is one that can be expanded to create a larger square table to seat four people for games and entertainment. A chair can be pulled from another room, the desk chair, and the two chairs from the bay window can be used to create the four chairs around the game table. This is a wonderful way to use multi-functional furnishing to accommodate various activities.

With this layout, we have also created four zones in one room!

1) A TV viewing zone with the sectional sofa and accent chair

2) A work zone with the desk

3) A reading zone with the two chairs in the bay window, and

4) A game zone once we expand the desk.

Wow, that's how to maximize space!

LAYOUT OPTION #1a

LAYOUT OPTION #1b

LAYOUT OPTION #2

This is another great layout which has even more seating, enough seats for 12 people. The sectional sofa seats five, the accent chair seats one, the game table seats four, the desk has two ottomans positioned underneath, that's a total of 12 seats.

However, with this layout, we've created three zones instead of four in one room. Even though we have fewer zones, we have more seating.

LAYOUT OPTION #2

LAYOUT OPTION #3

This layout has seating for 12 people. Each sofa seats three with a total of six, the accent chair seats one, the desk seats one, and the game table seats four.

This layout lends itself to a more formal style. It does not have seating that faces the TV directly. However, if TV viewing is one of the main activities for this space, it may not be the most comfortable option.

When selecting furniture options for TV viewing, keep in mind that every single seat in the room may not have the best viewing position. This is fine. Most times, it is not possible to have every seat be the 'best seat in the house.' Having the best seat for everyone may need to be saved for the theater room where the sole purpose is for TV watching.

LAYOUT OPTION #3

LAYOUT OPTION #4 (1 Zone)

Again, this is the layout I see most often in homes. It's very easy to think of a room as a single space and naturally begin to furnish it as such. However, in doing so, you will miss the opportunity to fully maximize the look, feel, and function of the room. It also has limited seating for a maximum of six due to its 'one-zone' layout. Take a look at Layout #4 verses Layout #2…

1 ZONE VS 4 ZONES

LAYOUT #4

LAYOUT #2

Wow, what a lost opportunity with a 'one zone' layout for a space that can comfortably create at least 3-4 zones and seating for 12 instead of 6. Although we are decorating for the number of family members for everyday use, this space can clearly handle seating for 12 without overfilling the seating plan.

Whenever possible, it's great to place or 'float' furniture inside the footprint of the room instead of against the wall. If there is at least one accent chair that can be placed across the main seating or sofa, this creates an arrangement that's more conducive to conversation. When you can create seating that allows people to sit across from each other, this creates a cozy, comfortable conversation experience that's much more welcoming.

I know furnishing a space can be expensive. This is another reason why a plan is so important. It is certainly possible to create 'high style on a budget,' and it's perfectly fine to purchase a little at a time. Doing so is an enjoyable experience and allows you time to live in the space and get a feel for how you'll truly use the space. Of course, this would apply to a space you have not occupied for long. But remember, don't leave a room empty for too long. Properly maximize what has been entrusted to you.

The order and layout of your space requires proper planning right from the start.

Just as there is an order to renewing our minds for Christ and maintaining a positive mental state, there is an order to creating the perfect layout for optimal use and maximum JOY in our homes!

✓ **Step 6 Interior Joy Check – Layout**

1. Is there a room in your home full of clutter or left empty? List three things you can do today to start the process of maximizing it?

2. Think of at least two room layouts you can create for the room you selected in step 1.

3. If you answered yes to question #1 about having a cluttered or empty room, pray. Do the 3R's and write what God tells you to do.

Step 7

'Wow Factor'
God's Principle

STEP 7

FAVOR

Genesis 39:2 *(NKJV)*

"The Lord was with Joseph, and he was a successful man, and he was in the house of his master the Egyptian. And his master saw that the Lord was with him and that the Lord made all he did to prosper in his hand. So Joseph found favor in his sight, and served him."

When I hear the word 'FAVOR,' it makes me smile! It's one of those words that conjures up feelings and visions of all things good. I even expand the word at times and think of the word 'flavor,' so visions of ice cream and decadent deserts begin to flood my mind. Okay... that may be a stretch. I just love to eat!

But, favor is something that comes as a gift, something good, extra, a surplus, and maybe even unexpected. From God, it's free with no strings attached.

However, favor also denotes that some type of relationship is in place. Something has occurred to attract it, some type of energy was expended, something was planted, a decision, a seed, an activity, or maybe some time given. Something of value has taken place in order to position you for favor.

God loves to bestow favor upon his children. God's favor is not for selfish gain but from selfless love.

Because Joseph had God's favor, God gave him extra favor through the eyes of the Egyptian master. Joseph, who was an Israelite, found favor even in the eyes of an Egyptian.

If you're a child of God, which by now I'm claiming you are, a decision has been made-the decision to allow God to be the Lord of your life. You are now positioned for God's Favor. When God's hand is on you, His favor is too!

Enjoy His extra hand of favor and yes, even more flavor for your life!

Step 7
'Wow Factor'
Décor Principle

STEP 7
DÉCOR 'WOW FACTOR'

Favor is that 'extra factor' that enhances your life, sometimes unexpectedly. It's that extra boost and blessing given that may help you achieve a goal or reach something desired. Well, that's exactly what happens in your home when you're able to incorporate that special added touch of 'Wow Factor.'

Most times, when working with clients, that's usually what's requested. They are looking for something different, some kind of 'wow factor' in their home.

'Wow factor' is that extra element in a space that conjures up a feeling of excitement, spontaneity, wonder, and even JOY! That element could be the color, the pattern, the size or just the item itself. The item could be a conversation starter, or just something that enhances a room's interest.

I believe every room should have some element of 'wow factor,',something of interest to take the design aesthetics up a notch. 'Wow factor' items are the attention grabbers in a space.

The beautiful thing is the item doesn't have to be expensive to have an impact. Something as simple as a tall glass vase with tall wooden stems or branches can create a sense of 'Wow.'

What creates the interest is the size or scale of the vase and branches. If placed in the center of a room on the coffee table, for instance, the arrangement breaks the line/plane of space in an area that's usually left empty in the center of the room. It's a focal point and draws the eye.

For example, in a typical space, there are 3 levels or planes of a room from the floor to the ceiling:

1. Lower plane

2. Middle plane

3. Highest plane

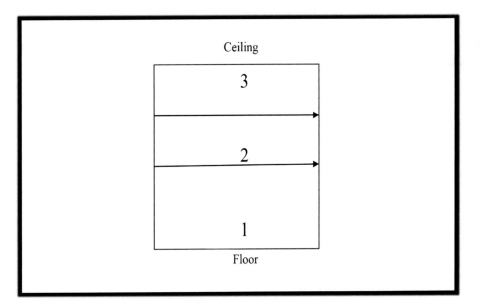

The lowest plane is where the furniture sits. The middle plane is where artwork may be hung. The highest plane is where the windows are located, and window treatments are hung.

In the center of a room, the middle plane is usually void of items with height.

Tall branches in a glass vase on the coffee table, for instance, 'break the plane' of space (Level 2) that's usually void. (See Image #1 and #2)

This is not an attempt to fill every space with décor. On the contrary, negative space is needed to allow the eye to rest. Every space on the wall, for instance, does not need to have an item on it. Knowing when to stop adding decor is just as important as knowing what to add and where to place it. Many times, less is more.

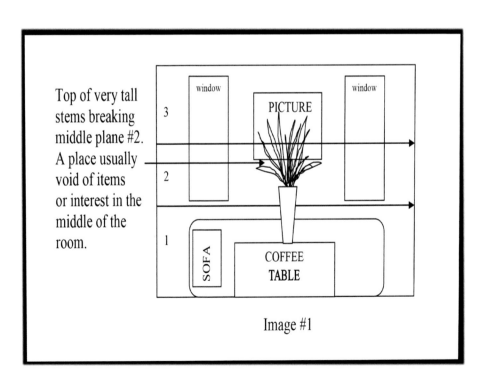

Image #1

IMAGE #2

There are many ways to add 'Wow Factor" to a space. Here is a list of 20 ideas to get the creative juices flowing.

1. Hang window treatments as high as possible above the window to bring the eye up, creating the feeling of a more expansive space. This helps to add interest to the level #3 plane.

2. Create a unique treatment on a focal wall. This can be paint, wallpaper or wood.

3. Large-scaled items are a great way to add wow-factor. It can be a picture, a vase, as mentioned earlier, a piece of metal art, or furniture.

4. Interesting flooring with a unique print or flooring arranged in an interesting pattern, such as wood flooring placed in a chevron pattern.

5. Paint a tall bookcase a fun 'pop color' like orange or tropical blue.

6. Use removable wallpaper to cover a dresser or chest and add fun knobs.

7. Create a four-poster canopy bed by hanging fabric from the ceiling to create the four-poster illusion.

8. Beautiful chandelier above coffee table in the living room or bedroom.

9. Paint your front door with an interesting color. Place the color on both the outside and the inside. Make the color part of your interior color scheme.

10. Replace your room door with a barn door adding interest and saving space.

11. Paint a console, a cabinet, or end tables a fun color. Let that particular item be the star! The color used should be repeated around the space sparingly, so the color items make the statement.

12. In addition to hanging the window treatments up as high as they will go, use a unique, bold pattern.

13. Create a beautiful wall collage of photos or pictures from magazines.

14. Paint the powder room with a fun, unexpected color.

15. Paint the ceiling a unique color, other than white.

16. Paint your kitchen cabinets and bathroom cabinets with a fun color.

17. Paint a unique focal point in your bedroom. Use a fun paint color to create a canopy effect behind and above your bed. Do this by painting a wide band of color behind the bed and take the color up onto the ceiling over the bed creating a canopy effect. This can even be done in lieu of using a headboard.

18. Use hanging pendant lights instead of lamps on the side table or nightstand.

19. Create a 'slim divider' as a column between two rooms. This is placed on each side of the door opening. Best if the door opening is wide. You can use carved Wood panels or create your own panels.

20. Paint the wood molding around your windows an accent color instead of using curtains.

Here is a room with lots of 'Wow Factor"!

It's all about your personal style and taste. The beauty of decorating your home is that it's yours. It should be as unique as your fingerprint. Remember…you are uniquely designed by God, and your space should reflect that. It doesn't matter if you rent, own, have a room or a mansion, there is a way.

The style of this space can be titled- "Eclectic Modern Throwback Chic." Create your own style and give it any name you please. Decorating should be fun and satisfying, not stuffy! In this room, there are elements from different design styles; Art Deco, Traditional, Mid-Century Modern, 'Afro-Centric' and Contemporary. Who knew there was such a style? If it's what you like in your home, then it's a-go. I happen to LOVE it!

This space highlights many of the 'Wow Factor' items we discussed.

- ✓ Unique wall color on the ceiling, not just white.
- ✓ Harmony and Flow of the gold accent color.
- ✓ Curtains hung high near the ceiling.
- ✓ Scale and proportion of furniture.
- ✓ Large scale mirrors for impact.
- ✓ Seating 'floated' across from each other, not all against the wall.
- ✓ Unique Accent wallpaper as a focal point.

This may not be your style but, it sure has 'Wow Factor'.

Let's take a look at our family room.

The 'Wow Factor' elements are:

- ✓ Bold print on the rugs
- ✓ Unique bamboo planter at the entrance.
- ✓ Nice furniture grouping
- ✓ Harmony and flow of cinnamon accent color.
- ✓ Chandelier lighting above the game table
- ✓ Large Scale wood-art above TV
- ✓ Curtains hung near the ceiling

Creating an atmosphere that nourishes you and your family should be an exciting one.

Go ahead, let your style shine through, and yes…you guessed it, your INTERIOR JOY too!

✓ **Step 7 Interior Joy Check – 'Wow Factor'**

1. Write the name of someone you can bless with 'favor' and share it over the next few weeks.

2. What 'Wow Factor" elements can you plan in your room from step 1?

3. Make a list of how God has shown favor in your life.

Step 8
Lighting
God's Principle

STEP 8

BE THE LIGHT

Being Ambassadors for Christ requires letting our light shine. If we are dim in an already dark place, there's no impact there. The joy that has been awakened within, as we put into practice the principles God has provided for our lives, should shine each and every day. Our interior joy should now be contagious inside and outside of the home!

Matthew 5:13-16 (NKJV)

"You are the light of the world. A city that is set on a hill cannot be hidden. Nor do they light a lamp and put it under a basket, but on a lamp-stand, and it gives light to all who are in the house. Let your light so shine before men, that they may see your good works and glorify your Father in heaven."

Have you ever met someone whose energy is contagious? I'm referring to positive energy because, unfortunately, negative energy can be contagious as well. Maybe it was their smile, a laugh, or their positive outlook on life. They are the person you may call when you are in need of sage advice or an opportunity to release some stress from a good joke or two.

Psalm 119:130 (NKJV)

"The entrance of your words gives light; it gives understanding to the simple."

It's difficult to live in a world that doesn't put God first. To be honest, I don't know how I lived without the enlightened word of God before turning my life over to Him. There are so many obstacles to maneuver that the thought of doing it alone seems daunting. Since making the right decision, I can truly see the difference.

The indelible impact He has made in my life is too obvious to deny!

I have so many powerful examples of God's impact on my life. The list is too long to capture here, but just to give you a taste of His power, I will tell you…He saved the life of one of my children who was literally two seconds from drowning, tuition scholarships for our kids, actually living dream vocation/careers, and teaching others how to do the same, making it through financial-storms, allowing me to write this book and so many more.

Psalm 27:1 (NKJV)

"The Lord is my 'light' and my salvation; Whom shall I fear? The Lord is the strength of my life; Of whom shall I be afraid?"

Light has a purpose, the greatest of which, of course, is allowing us to see. Not just physical sight but spiritual insight as well. As each new day brings an opportunity to connect to God, we'll emerge day by day out of the dark shadows that seek to choke us in this carnal world. The light becomes brighter, releasing the world's grip and opening the path to interior joy.

As a newly committed Christian or someone who is still unsure, God can sometimes seem a little esoteric, mysterious, or out of reach. However, God's word is not to be ingested in a day. It's a lifetime meal that starts with one decision and one bite at a time. Before you know it, your experience will be too obvious to deny. Be sure to set it on the hill of your life and let it shine!

Step 8

Lighting

Décor Principle

STEP 8
DÉCOR LIGHTING

Just as God's word is a lamp to your life's path, your home's lighting should illuminate its beauty and support all the activities that will take place. Lighting is one of those elements of décor; many people leave as an after-thought or give very little thought at all.

Our Design Plan

Step 1 - Room & Function	Family Room. Everyday living-Two adults. Two kids. No pets. family get-togethers, TV viewing, entertaining, napping, games, reading and, homework.
Step 2 - Style	Transitional
Step 3 - Mood	Casual Elegance
Step 4 - Color Scheme	Warm Gray, Tan, White, Cinnamon
Step 5 - Furniture	Sectional sofa, Accent chair, Coffee table, End tables, Desk, Game table with chairs, Accent chairs with table, Rug, Bookcase, Lamps.
Step 6 - Order/Layout	The furniture order/arrangement is determined by the function determined in step #1.

Step 7 - Wow Factor   Unique bookcase, flow of cinnamon
                             color, large scale TV stand.

Step 8 - Lighting

This step cannot be ignored. You can have the most beautiful decor with the best layout, but if the lighting is bad, the space will lack visual impact and function. As we continue to create our décor plan, Step 8 is lighting.

There are several types of lighting that should be considered.

Now… you may not incorporate every type of light in every room, but you must at least think it through. It's best to create your light plan in this order:

Three basic types of lighting:

1. General

2. Task

3. Accent/Mood

General lighting

It provides the overall light for the room. Some key forms of general lighting include recessed lights, ceiling light fixtures, and chandeliers. Typically, when you walk into a room and turn on the light switch, it should illuminate the entire room with balanced lighting. Other forms of general lighting may include floor lamps and soffit lights, which cast light onto ceilings and walls. Floor lamps can sometimes be used as task lighting as well.

Task lighting

It provides light for more specific purposes, such as reading with table lamps or desk lamps for working in an office. Also, pendant lights over a kitchen island and under-cabinet lights are ideal task lights for food prep and entertainment.

Accent/Mood lighting

Adds an additional touch to a space. Dimmers can be placed onto any light fixture to help set a mood, but generally, accent lighting is used to draw attention to a particular item. Examples may include picture lights above artwork, bookcase lighting, spotlights above a fireplace, or strip lights illuminating a path in a theater room.

Our "Wow Factor" room shows three types of lighting

    1. Ceiling recessed lights and fan- General lighting

    2. Floor lamp (in place of table lamp) - Task lighting

    3. Pendant lights near a focal wall- Serving as accent lighting above the consoles.

The correct lighting allows your home's décor to be seen as you intended. It also maximizes your ability to fully function in each room. A well-lit room definitely enhances the overall atmosphere and, of course your Interior Joy!

STEP 8: LIGHTING

✓ **Step 8 Interior Joy Check – Lighting**

1. Who has been a light in your life?

2. How can you be a light in the lives of others?

3. What form of lighting will you add to the space you selected in Step 1?

Step 9

Accessories

God's Principle

STEP 9

WHOLE ARMOR

God's spiritual armor protects the truth!

Truth be told, the enemy does not care as much about the physical you, as you may think; he's much more interested in your soul. If he gets the soul (that has not made the right decision), he's got the body and spirit to boot!

Soul - (Mind/Will/Emotions)-The essence of your personality.

Body - The physical self, the flesh.

Spirit - The heart of God.

Armor may be the last thing you put on, but it should be one of the first things you 'think on'.

What we think and feel ultimately controls what we say and do. Your mind, your will and emotions, whether right or wrong, works similar to a 'bit' used to control the direction of a horse. The rider pulls on the reign, which applies pressure to the 'bit' instructing the horse to go right, left, slow down, or stop. Just like a bit to a horse, your soul is to your decisions and direction.

How you operate in the world, before becoming a Christian, is decided by- the soul of you (mind, will, emotions). So, as a nonbeliever, the soul is leading the way. Whatever the soul wants, with all its fleshly desires, the body and spirit follows. Just what the enemy desires.

God created us in His likeness with the ability to choose. That freedom is powerful. Once sin entered the world, through disobedience (Genesis 3:6), we began to follow the flesh.

Operating in this physical world certainly has its challenges. To protect ourselves, we can sometimes get in God's way. We want to think of ourselves as being self-sufficient, advancing through the physical challenges of life, hardships, and disappointments, along with the responsibilities of school, children, work, and relationships. We're trying to do it all. In doing all this, it's easy to become distracted from the fact that we are operating in not just a physical world, but a spiritual one as well.

We are spiritual beings operating in the physical world.

The enemy gets a foothold when we forget the truth of what is happening all around us-behind the scenes. Every day, we wake up, the physical is obvious, but if we go too long without reminding ourselves of what's happening behind the scenes, we begin to operate only in the physical and forget about the spiritual. That's how we become overwhelmed with life, trying to do it all alone. In our physical world, there are many types of armor - hard hats, vests, knee pads, elbow pads, shoulder pads, steel toe shoes. All of these accessories are used to protect a certain part of the body. Each has a different look, size, and shape for its specific purpose. These are physical protectors providing temporary, limited coverage.

However, God has fully equipped us with powerful permanent protection. His internal, external, and eternal armor of protection. His Internal Holy Spirit External protection from surrounding supernatural powers and Eternal Salvation.

"The Whole Armor of God' allows us to fight the surrounding spiritual battles against principalities and powers of this Dark Age. (Ephesians 6:10-12)

God's armor protects what He has ordained. His truth.

Ephesians 6:10-17 (NKJV)

1) **Belt of Truth**
2) **Breastplate of righteousness**
3) **Gospel of peace**
4) **Shield of Faith**

5) **Helmet of Salvation**
6) **Sword of The Spirit**

1. The Belt of Truth- God's truth holding everything together, just like a belt. Covers the area of the body that houses loins and other internal organs.

2. The Breastplate of Righteousness – Protects your heart and righteousness through Christ.

3. Gospel Shoes of Peace-Be prepared and ready to move in this spiritual battle. Share the gospel with others.

4. Shield of Faith- In your left hand, hold your faith shield up against the fiery darts of the enemy.

5. Helmet of Salvation- God saves. Made you in His image and gave you the mind of Christ. It must be protected.

6. Sword of The Spirit- In your right-hand, holds the sword of God's Word. It's the power needed to defeat the enemy.

In this battle, we call life; God's armor covers every imaginable situation of all shapes and sizes. It's what we need to battle the truth of what's going on in and around us.

Don't leave home without it!

Step 9

Accessories

Décor Principle

STEP 9

DÉCOR ACCESSORIES

Just as God's spiritual armor is the layer for God's armor to protect the mind, body, soul, and spirit, your home's accessories are the final layers to enrich the soul of your home.

Accessories are those simple things that can sometimes be a little tricky to get the outcome desired. It can be a little frustrating trying to figure out exactly what to get and where to place each item.

You move into that beautiful, new home with two-story ceilings and ask yourself, what in the world will I put on that wall that seems to stretch forever. A mirror? Shelves? A picture? Or maybe two pictures? Oh…decisions, decisions!

When selecting accessories, consider the design style, color scheme, and overall mood of the space you're creating. Sometimes, it's an accessory that inspires the entire design plan from the beginning. A favorite piece of wall art or chair fabric you love may help determine the color scheme for the room. Although this can happen, most accessories are determined after the first eight steps are completed.

It's also a lot of fun to shop for accessories. Sometimes, in our excitement, we head out to the fabulous home stores and purchase all the 'pretty stuff' before the design plan is done. Please refrain from doing that to save yourself a lot of wasted money. It's important, when possible, to allow the final accessories to pull the space together and accent the room with 'wow factor.' When it's part of an overall plan, you can select just the right size, shape, color, and of course, price!

Some of the trade secrets to accessorizing a space are:

1. Place items in groups.
2. Use a minimum of three items as well as odd numbers in a grouping.
3. Group low, medium and tall items together.
4. Place 'collections' together in one place, when possible.
5. Select accessories with materials that support the design style of the room.
6. Use large-scaled items to enhance 'wow factor.' Large-scale not 'out-of- scale'.
7. Pay attention to scale and proportion. How an object relates to the items around it is important.
8. Don't over-do it. Walls need negative space to allow the eye to rest.
9. Hang wall art at a similar height around the room.
10. Consider round accessories to offset a lot of strong angles.
11. Accessories are a great way to add color and texture to a space, a nubby throw, furry pillow, or bright orange vase can be just what's needed.
12. Use accessories to add color flow around the room. A favorite color can be added in small touches around the room without overpowering the space.

Place Items In Groups of odd numbers

When placing items in groups of three or higher, odd numbers create a visual balance that is pleasing to the eye. It also keeps items from having a 'scattered', unorganized look.

Place Items at different levels

Using different heights enhances visual interest allowing the eye to move and appreciate the surrounding space.

Place 'like item' or collections together.

Placing your favorite collection of ceramic figurines or miniature cars in a localized area like a glass cabinet or family photos on a wall collage instead of scattered around the room, allows the viewer to appreciate the analogous relationship of all the items in the collection.

Select accessories made of materials that support the design style.

Here is an area that can sometimes cause frustration. Because there are millions of accessory options, trying to determine exactly what to choose can be daunting. One of the first things you should consider is; what is the item made of, and what is the material? For example, if you are creating a space with a modern theme, woven baskets may not be the best choice, but a sleek metal bowl would support the theme best. That woven basket would work great for your 'Farm-House-Rustic' décor theme. A paisley printed fabric on a chair would work best for a traditional or transitional look.

Can you mix items of different design styles? Of course, you can. Remember, this is your home and what you like-goes. However, these are general design concepts that serve as a 'guide' to increase your chances of achieving the best look for your space.

Use large-scaled items for 'Wow Factor'.

This is one of my favorite design tricks. Many open planned homes have walls that can reach two stories or more. These beautiful yet large spaces can pose a real problem for many homeowners. In this case, the wall accessories must be large and oversized. But, how about the smaller, cozier spaces? Are they restricted to lots of 'little' pictures and accessories? Absolutely not! Here is where a large-scaled mirror works great on a smaller wall! Now, things can still go awry if not done correctly, but in this setting, 'wow factor' is inevitable because it's unexpected and creates high impact.

Here, the large-scaled mirrors near the window look great!

Don't over-do it

Avoid the urge to place pictures on every wall and small accessories across every surface. Quality over quantity is a good rule-of-thumb. Now, when I say quality, higher-end price points are fine but, quality is not always about the price but the overall effect. A small grouping (various heights) of three items to one side and a buffet lamp on the other side of a long cabinet/console can be more effective than many items lined across the entire surface. Sometimes, 'less is more'!

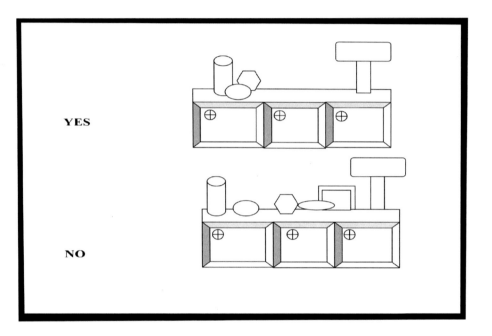

Let's take a look at a visual/mood board for our family room with the 'one zone' layout. We can enhance the décor by implementing the nine design principles we've covered so far. Let's also 'use what we have' and keep the sofa, love seat, and accent chair.

1. Room +Function	Family Room. Everyday users- Two adults. Two kids. No pets. Relaxed, Casual Fun. TV viewing, Napping, Games, Reading, Homework.
2. Style	Transitional
3. Mood	Casual Elegance
4. Color Scheme	Gray, Tan, Cinnamon
5. Furniture	Use original Sofa, Love seat, and Accent chair. Add Bench, Game table with chairs, Rug, Bookcase, Lamps, TV Unit, Side table, and accessories.
6. Layout	Two zones. 1.) TV viewing zone, 2.) Game and homework zone.

7. Wow Factor	Unique bookcase, flow of cinnamon color, large scale TV Stand.
8. Lighting	Ceiling fan, recessed ceiling lights, Table lamps
9. Accessories	Plants, candles, pillows, rug, wall art, magazine rack.

Visual Mood Board

A visual board or mood board is a wonderful tool to help you visualize all the furniture, accessories, and materials for your new design.

Here you see examples of our color scheme with the paint and fabric samples. We selected gray, tan, and accents of cinnamon. I like to use the term 'cinnamon' because it's not exactly orange or red but somewhere in-between.

We also have a nice variety of woods. Mixing different wood surfaces adds depth and interest. I prefer to mix woods and avoid the look of an exact match on all the furniture. We just need to make sure they complement each other.

The accessories go well with our 'Transitional' design style. Remember that is a mix of traditional and modern styling.

The mood is 'casual elegance' and the materials selected help to create this look and feel. Natural materials like warm wood tones evoke a casual feel while the smooth services of the glass and ceramics in the lamps and accessories help create elegance.

We also incorporated the color black as an accent as well as white in the lampshades and accessories for added interest and balance.

BEFORE

AFTER VIEW 1

AFTER VIEW 2

AFTER VIEW 3

✓ **Step 9 Interior Joy Check - Accessories**

1. In this season of your life, how can you put on the whole armor of God to assist you? List each piece of armor and write what it can do for a challenge you're facing today.

2. Now that you have 9 steps to your design plan, create a visual board for your new space.

3. What awakened Interior Joy for you in this step of the process?

Step 10

Budget

God's Principle

STEP 10

MAXIMIZE

God takes plans to the MAX!

We may sometimes become frustrated with life when it does not produce what we want when we want it. However, as we have learned, when we appreciate what's been entrusted to us and offer it back to God, we will witness how He can maximize it.

I've had to deal with the realization that I can have a perfectionist spirit sometimes. This is a definite block to what God wants to do in my life. Staying too focused on my plan causes procrastination and stagnation when things go wrong or move too slowly.

When we plan and focus in our own strength forgetting the promises of God, we have in-essence squeezed Him out and limited our ability, operating with a lack of faith. Doing so breeds fear,

135

doubt, frustration, and even arrogance. It's impossible to receive the maximum from God when we operate in our limited ability.

Matthew 17:20 (NKJV)

"So Jesus said to them, "Because of your unbelief, for assuredly, I say to you, if you have faith as a mustard seed, you will say to this mountain, 'Move from here to there, and it will move; and nothing will be impossible for you."

We must stop operating in self and give God something to work with, even a small seed of faith. After we give Him the seed, we must provide room for it to take root. That room can be time, patience, more prayer, reading His word, listening and most importantly, obedience! This provides good soil for God to work through.

Finally, in God's timing, He'll provide a step to take and you must take action! Just like the servants with the two and five talents. The entire plan may not be revealed right away, but that should not stop you from moving. You'll get the next step in His timing, not yours. If you have not gotten the next step, then there is something to finish on the last step. God will never leave you without a word. If you're feeling far from God and a little disconnected, guess who moved? Definitely, not God; He'll never leave you and is always there.

Reconnect and seek His guidance. His plans are so amazing; you can only handle a step at a time. Can God make things happen in an instant? Of course, but if that has not happened, focus on the most recent step He already provided.

In the end, when He maximizes the plan the view is as different as the image of an acorn versus an oak tree. He will enlarge, and infuse the situation with so much power you can't even imagine the results. Give God your seed of faith and listen for the next step to take.

Since we're on the topic of maximizing, right here is a wonderful time to discuss the tithe. God will maximize that 10% beyond measure. We are commanded to give of the first fruits from the top of our income. The very first, not second or leftovers, but the first 10% right off the top along with any offerings. If you want to know current life stories from the results of tithing, ask the Christians in your life who've been faithfully, consistently tithing over the years. They will have some stories to share, guaranteed! Your personal connections and true-to-life accounts with spiritual Christians in your life are invaluable.

Trust me when I say, God has maximized my seed of faith and tithes beyond measure. Some of what He has done in my life I've already shared. I'm not perfect; remember that's not what God is looking for, its attitude and obedience of the heart. So, go ahead… ask. Ask those you know and get ready to be blessed. What you hear will be an amazing experience of interior joy!!

Step 10
Budget
Décor Principle

STEP 10

DÉCOR BUDGET/SMART SHOP

Wow! Saving the best for last, we've been faithful with a little, maximized, and in position to be trusted with more. It's time for the reward of the fun stuff… smart shopping!

We have done things in decency and order, completing nine steps of our ten-step decorating process.

<u>Our Design Plan</u>

Step 1 - Plan & Function	Family Room. Everyday living two adults. two kids. No pets. Family get-togethers, TV viewing, entertaining, napping, games, reading and homework.
Step 2 - Style	Transitional
Step 3 - Mood	Casual Elegance
Step 4 - Color Scheme	Warm Gray, Tan, White, Cinnamon
Step 5 - Furniture	Sectional Sofa, Accent Chair, Coffee Table, End Tables, Desk, Game Table with Chairs, Accent Chairs with Table, Rug, Book case, lamps.
Step 6 - Layout	The furniture order or arrangement is determined by the function determined in Step #1.
Step 7 - Wow Factor	Highlights of your unique style.

Step 8 - Lighting	General, Task, Accent/Mood
Step 9 - Accessories	The final layer for maximum results.
Step 10-**Budget/** **Smart Shopping**	Oh what fun!

God's principle of maximizing most certainly applies here with our budget. How can we take what we have and maximize it to the fullest?

Now,…you may be asking, why is the budget the very last step? Why didn't we determine our budget in step number one? Well, I'm so glad you asked.

Remember the concept of operating in limits? Most of us, I will go ahead and assume, do not have unlimited budgets. Okay, I will speak for myself. My budget has a limit! However, my decor imagination does not.

'It's free to imagine'.

Placing the budget as Step #10 removes the limits from our creativity, allowing us the freedom to dream big from the start!

It's a wonderful thing to freely imagine our spaces, exactly as we want them to be. We may not get everything we imagine, but we certainly can maximize our dreams and fit them into our budget.

With all the wonderful, discount furnishing stores and websites available today, the sky's the limit!

FabuLESS

Million-dollar looks for less, 'FabuLESS' is within our reach. I love mixing high-end and low-end furnishings in my home. It's not being cheap; it's smart… smart shopping! I can think of many other ways to spend the extra $2,000 that's charged for a sofa that should cost only $1,500. I'm just say-in! Smart shopping and being responsible is how we honor God with the financial resources He has provided.

Some of my favorite stores include HomeGoods, HomeSense, T.J. Maxx, Marshalls, Tuesday Morning, Hobby Lobby, Ross. For on-line retailers, I love Overstock.com, LampPlus.com, Rugs-direct.com, and Wayfair.com, to name a few. There are great recycle stores and markets, along with model home clearance centers all over the country. I'm excited just thinking about them. I can spend all day just walking the isles or searching websites just looking at all the beautiful décor items available at great prices!

There is no reason to over-extend ourselves or to live in an atmosphere of lack. Remember, interior joy is achieved as we put God first, awakening our hearts joy, being grateful for what we have, which increases creativity in our homes, and honoring God.

Here are some fabuLESS ideas to accessorize your home:

1.   Take a beautiful silk scarf or old printed blouse that's no longer useful, cut it and frame it as art-work.

2.   Create 'no-sew' window treatments using a new table-cloth that has a pattern or color you like. Get the 108" rectangle table cloth. Because it has finished edges you only need to hot-glue the rod pocket opening by turning the fabric over 2" at the top, hot glue it and place the curtain rod inside. 108" is long enough for a window and ceiling height of 8 feet. You can either puddle the hem under at the bottom or cut and hot glue a hem. I have done this for many clients on a budget. They look awesome and last.

3.   Purchase inexpensive curtain panels from the store and add two of the same panels together to achieve a fuller, wider look. They will have the appeal of higher-end 'window treatments' instead of just basic curtains. If you need additional length, add a band of fabric at the bottom in a contrasting color.

4.   Use the pieces of the same fabric from your curtains to create a curtain tie-back. Embellish the tie backs with jewels or stones.

5.   Embellish a simple chandelier with your crystals you select.

6. Use large mirrors or canvas prints when possible to enlarge the look of a space. Add a new look and color to that frameless bathroom mirror by adding wood molding, cut and placed directly on top and around the edges of the mirror. You can even take a wide, sturdy, printed fabric ribbon and do the same.

7. Hang wall sconces (candle or electric) with pictures to create a large-scaled look on a wall without over-doing it with an excessive amount of pictures.

8. Use one of your special glasses, crystal or just a simple jelly jar and add some low cut fresh flowers from the grocery store. Fresh flowers are flowers no matter where you purchase them.

9. If you hate your floors and it's just not in the budget to replace them, reconsider…wait for it…stick on vinyl floor tiles. Now, if you're like me that would be the last thing I wanted. However, the flooring industry has come a very long way. You will be amazed at the options and the results. Even if it's a short term fix, it's so worth it!

10. Replace the wood spindles in your staircase railing with wrought iron spindles. Your local big-box retail stores have them in stock. This option is significantly less expensive than replacing the entire wood banister and the results are awesome! They look like jewelry on your staircase.

✓ Step 10 Interior Joy Check – Budget

1. If you have not done so, commit to tithe 10% and watch what God can do! If you have been tithing, what are two of the most recent blessings you've experienced?

2. For your space selected in Step 1, list three bargain-priced accessories to beautify your space.

3. Now that your decorating plan is complete and you are ready to 'smart shop,' record your Interior Joy experiences here.

Beautiful… but beautifully outdated. (For me.)

The Unlimited Dream

Interior Joy

This has been an amazing journey through God's principles and the steps of enhancing your home's décor, creating an atmosphere of gratitude and God's love. Decorating takes on a whole new meaning when it's purposed to honor God.

I am so blessed to have the opportunity to share this experience with you. As a professional Interior Decorator, it brings me great joy to open my heart and share the decorating expertise God has entrusted to me. It's been a goal of mine to write a book for several years. God insisted that I get it done! His plans are always greater than mine.

Following these ten steps will open your heart and home to the possibilities of God's amazing power and the *Interior Joy* He has planned specifically for you! I love you in the name of Jesus! Be Blessed!

1 Thessalonians 5:16 (NKJV)

"Rejoice always, pray without ceasing, in everything give thanks, for this is the will of God in Christ Jesus for you."

146

ABOUT THE AUTHOR

Charisse Holder is a woman of God who believes in the power of home.

She is the CEO of TRANSFORMATIONS Home and Life and a Certified Interior Decorator. Charisse has facilitated focus-study courses at her home church First Baptist Church of Glenarden, taught continuing education classes at Prince Georges Community College, and she mentors budding Entrepreneurs and Interior Decorators through her 'Décor-Mentor' mentorship workshops. She has an extreme passion for encouraging others to uncover their gifts and live their best life.

Charisse discovered her natural talent for Interior Decorating at the age of 25 when she purchased her first townhome in Sicklerville, New Jersey. Decorating brought such joy that it planted a seed of God's destiny for her life. Fifteen years later, her decorating business was born.

Raised by her beautiful Mom, Katie, with her two siblings Melissa and Yvette, Charisse remembers home being beautiful, tidy and welcoming. It had to be tidy because Katie established early on that, every single Saturday morning was 'clean the house time'! No exceptions. There are memories of her Mom's amazing decorating skills where custom window treatments and upholstered sofa covers were beautifully crafted by Mom herself. She maximized what she had at all times, making everything look and feel abundant. As a single parent to three girls, her life was not easy; however, life for her and her children was full due to her resourcefulness and God's grace. It was clear that – home mattered! This book is dedicated to Mom!

Charisse truly believes… Everyone deserves a beautiful space to call home. No matter the size of the space, knowing God's truth can transform any situation. Her mission is to help others- particularly women- feel the joy of what has been entrusted to them. What's in possession- right now- can be used to transform your spaces into a home that honor God, which awakens true 'Interior Joy.'

Charisse has been married over 23 years to her husband, N. Louis Holder, M. Ed. She has two children, Jordan Louis and Jasmine Rena Delores. She resides in Bowie, Maryland.

Thank you for reading this book. It was a project from the heart. If you enjoyed reading it, please share a few sentences of your experience on Amazon. I pray to touch as many lives as possible.

To get more information about other products and services, please visit us at:

www.TransformMeNow.org

www.InteriorJoy.net

Made in the USA
Middletown, DE
06 July 2020

11204721R00097